BOOKS BY SELMA R. WILLIAMS

KINGS, COMMONERS, & COLONISTS
Puritan Politics in Old & New England
1603-1660

DEMETER'S DAUGHTERS
The Women Who Founded America
1587-1787

RIDING THE NIGHTMARE
Women & Witchcraft
from the Old World to Colonial Salem

DIVINE REBEL
The Life of Anne Marbury Hutchinson

RIDING
THE
NIGHTMARE

*Women & Witchcraft
from the Old World to
Colonial Salem*

Selma R. Williams

AND PAMELA WILLIAMS ADELMAN

RIDING
THE
NIGHTMARE

---

*Women & Witchcraft
from the Old World to
Colonial Salem*

ILLUSTRATED WITH OLD ENGRAVINGS
AND PAINTINGS

HarperPerennial
A Division of HarperCollins*Publishers*

To Burt and Wendy

· Contents ·

List of Illustrations

THE UNTOLD TALE

Witchcraft is history's gothic novel—a medley of sex, murder, and encounters with the Devil.

Eerily, nonsensically, the story continues to blind writers to its most sensational aspect, the mass killing of women, in part, at least, as a way of denying women political and economic power. Historians by the hundreds have described the horrors while ignoring the victims. Scarcely a word or question can be found on the consistent choice of females for burning at the stake or hanging on the gallows.

This totally uncoordinated, though murderous, war on women forms the theme of *Riding the Nightmare*. The title refers to the *incubus* (male demon, frequently symbolized by a broomstick) or night-mare on which women were believed to ride through the air at night, in order to arrive at the gathering or *sabbath* of witches.

Such superstition and folklore are part and parcel of this book—as are the images of women in art and on the printed page.

A brief prologue sets the doom-filled stage for the book, contrasting the attitudes of the ancient world, which revered woman as a goddess, and the Middle Ages, which reviled her as a witch.

Part I covers the arrival of the Devil in Europe, for which women were eventually and almost exclusively blamed. Included here are the legendary and Biblical roots of the Great Witch Hunt, which occurred amidst the painful upheaval from medieval to modern life. The route of the Hunt is followed as it progresses through Western Europe, becoming sufficiently virulent to cross the English Channel in the second half of the sixteenth century.

Occupying an Interlude all by herself is Lilith, Adam's rebellious first wife. Chronologically she fits in everywhere and yet nowhere. Her demands for equality and subsequent banishment from Eden were legendary. With the Great Witch Hunt of the sixteenth and seventeenth centuries, witchcraft writers assigned her a new role: queen of the *succubi* (female demons), attacking by night.

Part II describes witch hunting in Britain, with special attention to the immediate effects on Puritans preparing to cross the ocean to the New World and the later influence on colonists long established in Massachusetts.

Scapegoats in Salem, Part III, reveals the Massachusetts outbreak in 1692 as a witch hunt in miniature, and thus an excellent case study for investigating the preponderance of women among witches. The proceedings are sufficiently concentrated in time (less than six months), space (one county, one courthouse), and numbers (141 accused, 31 convicted, 20 put to death), to examine why accusers were mostly men, accused mostly women.

Pictures of sculpture, paintings, and drawings illuminate the West's use of identical reasons for excluding women from power and for executing them as witches. Art both reflected and affected society—much as television does today. Preceding each chapter is a picture from the period, frequently supplemented by a relevant poem, story, or diatribe to help the reader enter into the mood of the times. Additional illustrations and source material appear throughout the book.

· *Prologue* ·

THE GODDESS
AND THE WITCH

An ancient Western earth mother, the Minoan snake goddess
from Crete, circa 1600–1500 B.C. The awe of early man for
motherhood and the earth glows in the closely related symbols
of the bare breast and the snake. The breast sustains life. The
snake, whose home is the ground, renews life periodically,
shedding its old skin to uncover the new skin beneath.—
COURTESY MUSEUM OF FINE ARTS, BOSTON

For thousands of years the West had adored the Earth Mother. Every culture—whether Minoan, Greek, Roman, or Germanic—gave its own special name to this goddess. But always she was responsible for the wonders of the world: food, clothing, children, peacefulness.

Some sculptors portrayed every one of her virtues in images no bigger than the size of a human hand (this Minoan snake goddess from Crete is only six-and-one-half inches high, for example). Others showed her as a giant—her hair, face, and body instantly recognizable as humanly inspired, but her massive stature evoking awe rather than familiarity.

Poets sang her praises with lyrics making Earth forever maternal, majestic, and miraculous—even today. In fact, the verse that follows, written some 2700 years ago, could well be the theme song of twentieth century environmentalists:

To Earth, Mother of All

Earth who is mother of all shall I sing on your noble foundation.
Eldest are you and you feed everything that exists in the world, all

*Those that inhabit the glorious surface of the earth and the
deep sea,*

*Plus those that fly in the air—they are fed, every one from
your bounty!*

*By you are excellent children and fruitfulness brought to
perfection,*

*Lady, there lie in your hands both the giving of life and the
taking,*

*Where mortal men are concerned. He is happy whom you in
your humor*

*Willingly honor, for everything then will be his in abun-
dance.*

*For him the vegetable furrow is fertile, and throughout his
pasture*

*Livestock are thriving, his home overflows with the prosperous
takings.*

—*Homeric Hymn, Greece, sometime before* 700 B.C.

TURNING THE SITUATION around completely, the Middle
Ages toppled woman from Earth Mother to witch. The process
was a slow one, taking at least a thousand years, from around
500 to 1500 A.D. And as generalizations go, there were many
times when equality between the sexes seemed at hand, or just
beyond the next turn of events.

Thus, in the centuries before 1000 A.D., the visible, earth-
dwelling Mother Abbess came to replace the mythical, unseen
Earth Mother. As Christianity began making deep inroads on
paganism, double monasteries of nuns and monks sprang up
all over Western Europe, each ruled with a firm hand by a
Lady Abbess. Reflecting this development, the English monk
and historian known as Venerable Bede immortalized a
woman named Hilda of Whitby: "The Abbess Hilda was
called Mother by all her acquaintances," he wrote. "So great
was her prudence that not only ordinary folk, but kings and

princes used to come and ask her advice in their difficulties and take it." Five men trained under her direction later became bishops—"all of them men of outstanding merit and holiness." Contemporaries wrote of many other women in France, Germany, and England who similarly exercised strong control over double monasteries. And beyond doubt, the authority relegated to the Lady Abbess tinged women with divine perfection.

Sometime around 1000 A.D., the institution of the Lady Abbess disappeared. The idea that women could successfully wield great power remained very much alive, however. As Europe moved to organize itself into nations rather than tribes, queens as well as kings covered themselves with glory in the political arena. One example was Eleanor of Aquitaine (1122–1204) who dominated English politics and history for most of the twelfth century."*

But by the 1300s things began visibly going downhill for women. Slowly but surely the stereotype of the evil-breathing old witch overwhelmed the image of woman as benign Earth Mother, Lady Abbess, or effective queen.

As society moved from open field to clustered community, man and woman ceased working together, side by side. Organization, authority, and power gradually slithered into the domain of man alone, reinforced finally by hundreds of thousands, maybe millions, of executions for witchcraft.

A witch was the Devil's agent and death's handmaiden, who could kill and destroy by supernatural means. She rode through the air on a broomstick at night over hundreds, sometimes thousands, of miles to meet with her witch cronies and to get further instructions from her employer, the Devil. This

---

* An excellent source for further information is Andrée Lehmann's *Le Rôle de la Femme au Moyen Age,* especially pp. 249–359. See bibliography for full listing.

Portrait of a witch. From a seventeenth century English chapbook.
—COURTESY BRITISH LIBRARY

conclave, or sabbath, brewed destruction that rained down on society—no community could escape wholesale death by famine, plague, or war; no man could protect his crops from ruination, his livestock from dying; no sailor at sea could hope to avoid death-laden storms; and no woman could be assured of safe childbirth.

Ordinary law was no match for the supernatural powers of a witch, even when she was trapped and imprisoned. She could, after all, bewitch her inquisitors or judges into setting her free. The only solution was to ignore the law and establish special rules substituting wild accusation for sober proof. All the ancient philosophers and the Bible itself gave strong support to such procedure. Especially in times of crisis, when the Devil threatened the end of the world, the only way to purge society of evil was to execute witches. Burning them to death was preferable, to get rid of every last trace of wickedness in their bones and bodies. But old and New England continually insisted on mere hanging.

Once the idea of witchcraft was accepted, singling out a witch was easy, even if she was never actually caught in her evil activities, and never seen riding that broomstick, or conferring with her co-workers. First of all, at least half the population was immediately suspect: as wise King James of Scotland and England would write at the turn of the seventeenth century, for every twenty-one witches, twenty were women. This was not surprising. There was something otherworldly about women, who had the ability to produce a live human being from within their own bodies, something no man, not even a king, could do.

Secondly, the Bible made the West's first woman, Eve, synonomous with lust and temptation, and advised, "Thou shalt not suffer a witch to live."

Thirdly, a witch's appearance exposed her. At a time when most women died before the age of forty, she was still going strong in her fifties, sixties, or even her seventies. She was too old to bear more children and so was no longer any use to society. And if she was near-sighted, or deaf, or bed-ridden; or if she limped, or stuttered, or was stoop-shouldered, she was especially to be feared rather than protected. Why then share scarce food or fuel with such a frightening-looking old hag who was hanging on only to do the Devil's bidding?

Midwives made up another whole group of witches. If a midwife could bring both mother and child safely through the throes of childbirth, she doubtlessly was calling on the supernatural. On the other hand, if either mother or child died, the midwife-witch was demonstrating her unearthly power for evil.

As for women who dared to assert themselves, they certainly deserved execution for witchcraft. After all, they were behaving contrary to history, the Bible, and the generally accepted inferiority of females to males in mental capacity and physical strength.

In the absence of science and scientific knowledge, superstition reigned supreme. Men acted on what they believed, what they had been told and taught over the centuries—not on what they could prove.

HERESY AND WITCHCRAFT

Born in the brooding Alps at the center of blindly staggering
Europe, a sect of religious heretics looked beyond the Church for
salvation. Known as Waldensians, they came to be labeled witches
by 1450. In fact, the very name Waldensian was used as a
synonym for the word witch.

    Johannes Tinctoris, a retired professor of theology and rector
of Cologne University, helped spread their reputation for
wickedness with a manuscript warning Western Europe of fatal
chaos should Waldensians ever gain control:

Against the Sect Which is Called the Waldensians

Indeed, then no one will follow tradition, obey the law, respect justice or show concern for life. Nor will there be any defense or protection for the state, or love or respect for God. Everything will be turned upside down in confusion; every winner will set his own rules and will subvert all government.—TRANSLATION FROM THE LATIN MANUSCRIPT *Contra Sectam Valdensium,* PUBLISHED AT TOURNAI, BELGIUM, 1460.

This illustration of a witches' sabbath, used with the manuscript by Tinctoris, combines all the elements found in popular fantasy up to the mid-fifteenth century. Waldensian heretics ("witches") are gathered together to worship the Devil in the shape of a he-goat. The founder of the sect, Peter Waldo, in 1173, had asserted that women should be allowed to preach along with men. Thus both men and women are present, and all reveal membership in the upper class by their expensive clothes and the castle in the background. For transportation to their meeting place, they fly through the air on the back of a monstrous beast.
—PICTURE COPYRIGHT BIBLIOTHÈQUE ROYALE, BRUXELLES

CHAPTER ONE

Turmoil in the West

The end of the world was due any time after 1300. Death stalked every family, everywhere, every day. An unknown poet sang:

> *With weeping we come*
> *And so pass away*
> > *In pangs we start,*
> > *In pangs we end*
> > *In dread we stay*
> > *And in dread depart.*
>
> *Consider, man, how you should go,*
> *And study in what plight you're thrown:*
> *In filth you're sown, in filth you grow,*
> *And worms shall eat you for their own.*
> *Three days of bliss you've hardly known*
> *On earth, and all your life is woe.*

The bubonic plague or Black Death, 1347–1351, killed one out of every three Europeans, striking particularly hard at the crowded cities—and then changing into an unending series of epidemics. At the same time, there was the bloody chaos of the One Hundred Years War between France and England, 1337–1453, fought in the accepted medieval manner of allowing soldiers to live completely off the land, forcing civilians to give up even meager food and shelter to defenders as well as invaders. Throughout the period, the Church was floundering helplessly, with the papacy forced to flee from Rome to Avignon, France, 1308–1378, only to return to the Rome of the Great Schism, 1378–1417, when two or three rival popes claimed authority.

Those who survived disease, war, and natural disaster faced the threat of slow death from starvation. There was simply not enough food to feed everyone. Beginning around 1300 and lasting well into the 1400s, an unexplainable change in weather brought violent storms and crop-destroying rains that caused a killing famine. London's Thames River and the Po River in the north of the Italian peninsula froze over for weeks or even months. And the herrings in the sound between Denmark and Sweden stopped spawning because of changes in the ocean circulation sometime around 1430.

As the earthly personification of Mother Nature, women were blamed for raising storms on land and sea, causing drought or flood, producing excessive heat or cold. Typical of countless stories was the one about an unnamed woman in Switzerland who confessed in 1359 to having attended an assembly of witches presided over by Satan (attending in the shape of a black cat). Satan, she recounted, taught the women to whistle a special way three times in order to cause snow, frost, and cold, which would ruin the crops of the valley.

Also making life miserable were the unaccustomed noise and stench of new industry. An anonymous fourteenth century poet complained about a nearby iron forge:

> *Swart smutted smiths, smattered with smoke,*
> *Drive me to death with din of their dints* [*blows or*
> *strokes*].

Robbing society of hope for the future, infant after infant died at birth. There was no obvious reason for these deaths, so surely some sinister force must be at work. The Middle Ages blamed first one out-group, then another: Jews, beginning around 1100; and women, sometime afterwards.

Jews, it was said, murdered babies to obtain blood for the Passover meal, part of their annual spring feast. And women who were witches killed and then devoured babies or small children at night. Well into the 1500s, Jews and witches were thrown into the deadly fire, at adjacent marketplaces, often on the same day. But as the 1500s moved on, the primary emphasis shifted to witches—especially since most Jews had been driven to take refuge in Eastern Europe.

Pointedly stressing the connection between anti-Christian Jews and Devil-worshipping witches, two terms borrowed from Judaism were used to describe witch assemblies. "Synagogue" was newly defined as the sacrilegious meeting with the Devil, and later the "sabbath" was such a gathering, usually occurring on Friday night or Saturday (though at some times or places any night of the week could be sabbath night).

Men were convinced that women eagerly attended sabbaths, under the watchful direction of the Devil, to teach their exclusively female apprentices the miracles of pregnancy and the techniques of infant birth and death. Actually, of course, it was the most natural thing in the world for women to help sisters, daughters, cousins, and neighbors before, during, and after pregnancy and delivery. Inevitably, some serviced strangers as well, proclaimed themselves midwives, and threw in a good-sized dose of mumbo-jumbo—extremely beneficial to their reputations and their pocketbooks if all went successfully. Miscarriages, hemorrhaging, and stillbirths were frighteningly common, so expectant mothers anxiously turned to midwives for charms or superstitious ceremonies.

When the infant and mother came through in good health, the midwife was a miracle worker. But when death resulted for the infant, or for the mother, or for both, midwives found themselves among the first to be labeled Satan's earthly agents.

Soon thrown into the same category were religious heretics, who looked beyond the established Church for hope and salvation.

THE CHURCH VIEWED WOMEN as the weaker sex, mentally and morally, and descended from Eve the temptress. Not surprisingly, then, the Church exaggerated the female role in the two leading heresies of the time, the Cathars and Waldensians, forerunners of the later Protestants.

Both sects, though they had strong masculine hierarchies, had opened their ranks to women in the late twelfth century— allowing them to preside over the eucharist, baptize, and pronounce absolution. But by the fourteenth century, Cathar writings began downgrading the role of women, and around 1321, several Cathar heretics, under severe persecution by the Church, embroidered their confessions with legends portraying women as Satan's tool for destroying men. As for the Waldensians, they increasingly relegated women to conventional roles: preparing the wine for the eucharist and serving the food at church suppers.

The Church ignored the diminished role of women in the heresies. And despite the view of women as the weaker sex, the Church directed harsh persecution against females as well as males, in order to extract confession and assure penitence. Both sexes were beaten, whipped, and subjected to inhumanly long imprisonment. Once accused, persons were considered guilty and had to prove their own innocence. Almost to insure that injustice would be done, the accused had no lawyer. Lawyers had been allowed in the beginning, but too often they were charged with guilt by association, or of outright involvement in the defendant's crime, so that before too long even the pretense of counsel was dropped.

The single concession to women was the papally approved decree, in 1376, that pregnant females were not to be tortured, out of fear of aborting the fetus.

IN THE 1300s AND 1400s frightening tales drifted in from the East in the wake of the Crusades (1096–1296), which further convinced Church and society of the need to exclude females from all participation in power. New versions of ancient myths and legends told of the Amazons, fearless female warriors and conquerors; Circe who changed men into pigs; Medusa who turned them to stone; Lilith, Adam's first wife, who demanded equality, deserted when it was denied, and forever after haunted all men as a night monster; Medea who killed her own sons to punish her husband. Women were obviously not to be trusted.

So the West began creating new versions of old legends, calculated to make women look foolish in their attempts to exert power. For example, the Chester mystery players of England, entertaining local villagers by presenting the Bible as folk drama, *c.* 1375, caricatured Mother Noah, portraying her in mock terror as a force to be reckoned with:

MOTHER NOAH: In faith, Noah, I would rather you slept
Than all this silly fussing.
I will not do what you have bid.

NOAH: Good wife, do now as I thee tell.

MOTHER NOAH: By Christ, no! till I see more need
Though thou stand all the day raving.

NOAH: Lord, all women be crabbed. Aye!
And never are meek, that I dare say.
This is well seen on earth today
Which witness you, each one.
Good wife, stop all this trouble and jeer
That thou makest standing here.
For all men think thou art my master
And so you are, by St. John

With the hindsight of the twentieth century, it is easy to see that these were years when massive change was taking place. Worship of money was replacing reverence for earth. Trade and commerce were becoming more important, and agriculture—and with it Mother Earth—were losing their ascendency.

Sometime in the late Middle Ages the seventeen books of
Strabo appeared, brimming with information of the ancient world,
some of it terrifying:

> Who could believe that any army of women, or a city,
> or a tribe, could ever be organized without men, and not
> only be organized, but even make inroads upon the territory
> of other people?—STRABO, *Geography,* CIRCA 21 A.D.

Off and on, memories of the Amazons had been frightening
men for thousands of years. Following the Crusades to the East,
1096–1296, they reappeared first in legend, then in art—though
few examples have survived the rigors of time.

This rare Flemish tapestry (late fifteenth century) was most
likely commissioned to grace the wall of some wealthy noble's
home. It glorifies Artemis Orthia ("Artemis the Upright" in
Greek and the alter ego of the Roman Diana), goddess of the
Amazons, and her two fearless daughters, Hippolyte and
Melanippe, fighting the strong Greek warriors, Hercules and
Theseus. Orthia appears in the center, sitting in an arched balcony
reminiscent of a temple or shrine. Her crown is the most elaborate
headdress of all the women present—everyone, incidentally,
dressed in medieval costume and so relating the ancient world to
the fifteenth century scene. —COURTESY ISABELLA STEWART
GARDNER MUSEUM, BOSTON

CHAPTER TWO

The Lady and the Saint

Medieval man had no difficulty recognizing independent women as latter-day Amazons and thus fuel for burning in the marketplace—a warning to others similarly inclined.

Two of Europe's most famous society-shakers, aristocrat Alice Kyteler, 1324, and peasant Joan of Arc, 1430, went on trial for their lives. They were persecuted for insubordination, but officially prosecuted for heresy and witchcraft. These two women have been discussed from every conceivable point of view—except in terms of the female struggle for political and economic participation.

Lady Alice Kyteler, a tough, female member of the Anglo-Norman aristocracy, was the first witch ever discovered in Ireland. As in later witchcraft trials, the court record—full of age-old horror tales, folklore, and superstition—barely reflected the actual reasons for persecution. Accordingly, at the trial in Kilkenny, Ireland (part of England's domain in the fourteenth century), a long parade of witnesses left no terror to the imagination. Explicitly they testified to Lady Alice's heresy, sorcery, and witchcraft, as well as petty treason, defined at the time as husband-murder.

She had denied Christ and refused to attend church, they insisted. Fiend that she was, her private recipe to harm enemies called for boiling together in the skull of a beheaded robber the entrails of cocks, spiders, serpents, and the brain of an unbaptized baby, as well as the nails and hair of corpses. In fact, this was how she had caused the unnatural deaths of some of her four husbands and had made her present husband, John le Poer, dangerously ill.

Lady Alice Kyteler's supposed recipe was freely borrowed from Pamphile, a wondrous woman with supernatural powers who appeared in Roman writer Apuleius's second century work, *The Golden Ass:*

> First, she prepared in this deadly workshop all her usual tools: every kind of aromatic herb, metal plates engraved with hieroglyphs, bones of ominous birds, assorted oddments from the graves of men who had died and who had wept and been buried; here, noses and fingers; there, the blooded nails of the crucified; and there, the blood of slaughtered men or the skulls removed from the jaws of wild beasts.
>
> Chanting over yet-palpitating entrails, she made sacred liquid with various ingredients—now with spring water; now with cow's milk; now with mountain-honey and mead. Then she plaited the goat's hairs, and twined them into a love-knot, and burned them odorously on live coals.

Lady Alice Kyteler's accusers knew well how to use witch lore and having set the stage, they then put forth the real causes for complaint against the Lady. First, they claimed that she had bewitched her husbands before their deaths into making her wealthy and powerful with generous gifts of property. Here she had worked with her incubus or demonic lover called Robin, who appeared at various times as a cat, a shaggy dog, or a black man.

This idea of "generous gifts of property" comes shrieking from the report of the trial. Lady Alice's multiple marriages

The theme of the demon lover, so often reported by word of mouth, and described in detail at the trial of Lady Alice Kyteler, would further circulate in the form of a picture, after the introduction of the printing press. —ILLUSTRATION FROM *De Lamiis* (CONCERNING WITCHCRAFT) BY ULRICH MOLITOR, 1489. COURTESY HARVARD THEATRE COLLECTION

certainly were not at all unusual (within months or even weeks of bereavement the surviving spouse customarily took a new mate). But her ownership of property, since she was a married female, was at best a fast disappearing holdover from Anglo-Saxon law and custom. Increasingly in Britain, the marriage ceremony turned a wife into a *feme couvert,* so that she was henceforth "legally dead" and could neither inherit nor possess land in her own name. In direct contradiction, the much-widowed but still married Lady Alice was the wealthiest inhabitant of Kilkenny. Her conviction for witch-heresy would allow confiscation and redistribution of her holdings.

This one strong clue to the real reasons for Lady Alice's troubles leads to uncovering others—which in turn reveal half-hidden angles that obviously changed the entire direction and outcome of the case. (1) The prosecutor for the Irish court is a Londoner: William Ledrede, a French-trained Franciscan acting in accord with recently issued papal bulls against heresy and sorcery. (2) His allies are a wide array of English knights and nobles directing the drive to control Ireland. Nurtured on feudal ideals of masculine strength and supremacy (necessary for war and conquest), all are firmly convinced that, in the intense struggle being waged by the English monarchy to subdue the Celts of Ireland, property is power that properly belongs in male hands only. (3) The local Celtic population look on Lady Alice as a rank outsider, just one more member of the despised occupying force.

Consequently, Lady Alice could find few allies anywhere. And outspoken female supporters were burned at the stake, a warning to others. Even Lady Alice's servant, Petronilla of Meath, who—after six public floggings—proclaimed her mistress the outstanding practitioner of ritual magic in the whole world, was put to death.

But fearlessly, Alice Kyteler stood up for her own rights. When Ledrede ordered her excommunicated, she retaliated by denouncing him for defamation of character and attempted to force his appearance before the parliament in Dublin. The more powerful Ledrede won the contest, however, causing the Lady to flee for her life to England where she disappeared into invisibility.

Lady Alice's stepchildren had actually set the entire persecution in motion. She was, after all, related to her stepchildren only through marriage to their now dead fathers, and substantial amounts of property had been left to her and her alone by each husband—to the exclusion of his own offspring. In other words, here was a situation ready made to produce a scapegoat. Burn this *prima donna* for heresy and witchcraft, and both society and particular individuals would be rid of all the evil she was producing.

WITH ALICE KYTELER it was money and property. In an even more famous example one hundred years later, it was political power that brought the cry "witch." That woman was Joan of Arc (1412–1431). On her own, she had turned the tide of the Hundred Years War in favor of her native France and against the English invaders, 1429–1430. "False enchantments and sorcery" were her methods, contended the English Duke of Bedford, following her success in raising the siege of Orléans in the early days of May, 1429. Two months later, on July 17 at Reims, she crowned Charles VII king, settling the bitter contest for the throne of France raging between supporters of Henry VI of England and Charles.

Brimming with confidence, enthusiasm, and superhuman energy, she was the stuff that legends are made of (in fact, the number of writings on Joan is estimated at over five thousand).* She herself led troops into battle (and was twice wounded), imposed discipline on a previously defeatist and pillaging army, and inspired strong morale among both the soldiers and the people of the countryside.

Captured in battle on May 23, 1430, she might have escaped—except that by a devious turn of events some of her own countrymen betrayed her in return for payment of 10,000 francs. She was made to face a court whose judges were either Englishmen or Frenchmen allied with England against their native land. And the shilly-shallying Charles VII, though for-

---

* Especially recommended is the account written by Regine Pernoud, *Joan of Arc, By Herself and Her Witnesses,* translated by Edward Hyams. The book relies extensively on primary source material, carefully translated from medieval French.

ever indebted to her for his crown, refused to come to her aid. Two women who did so were burned at the stake.

Her success against the English was the underlying—and purely political—reason for her persecution. Again, as in the case of Alice Kyteler, the trial record reflects only subtly the real reasons for Joan's persecution. All accusations against her were couched in terms of heretical behavior: wearing male clothing and sporting short hair; insisting that she was answerable directly to God for her words and deeds, not to the Church; falsely denying that she had been trained in the arts of witchcraft by neighbor women at her peasant home in Domremy, or that the voices that had impelled her actions were those of evil spirits.

Instead, she maintained that the voices were those of St. Catherine, St. Margaret, and the Archangel St. Michael.

Her choice of saints is highly significant. The legend of St. Catherine must have given needed courage to Joan in her own martyrdom—and at the same time frightened men with a reminder of female strength. At an unknown date in ancient time, the beautiful, intelligent Catherine of Alexandria refused the marriage proposal of the pagan emperor Maxentius, instead defending her Christian faith. Imprisoned, she was visited by a vision of Jesus, and when the authorities attempted to break her on a spiked wheel (a torture instrument since called the "Catherine wheel"), the wheel shattered, leaving her unharmed but killing several spectators who were hit by splinters. In the end, she was beheaded, calling out blessings to all who promised to keep her memory. From her severed veins milk, not blood, flowed. As for St. Margaret, she was said to have been swallowed by Satan disguised as a dragon. And St. Michael was the Archangel who protected soldiers.

Joan of Arc herself was kept in a dreary dungeon for one year plus one week, May 23, 1430 to May 30, 1431. For most of the time, she was chained by the neck, arms, and feet to a wooden block. Occasionally, she was locked in heavy irons.

Threatened with torture to make her confess, she retorted:

> Even if you tear me limb from limb, and even if you
> kill me, I should not respond otherwise; and if I did
> speak otherwise, I should always thereafter say that you
> had made me answer so by force.

At her trial, anything favorable to Joan was omitted from
the court record, when the French words actually used were
translated into official Latin. According to his own later testimony, the scribe Guillaume Manchon was forced by the
judges "to change the meaning of words." And, he added at
her posthumous trial for rehabilitation in 1459—by which
time he had reached the mellow age of sixty-one—that two
men hidden behind a curtain, near the judges, "wrote and reported what was charged against Joan and suppressed her
excuses."

Amazingly, under these circumstances, no one thought it
necessary to tamper with her most politically potent declara-
tion. Asked why she instead of another had been chosen as
savior of France, she explained matter-of-factly:

> Because it pleased God, by a simple maid, to drive out
> the enemies of the King.

At the age of nineteen, Joan was led to the stake, the mitre
on her head covered with the words "relapsed heretic, apostate,
idolater." The torture continued to her very last breath. She
was placed on an uncommonly high pile of wood so that the
flames would be slow to consume her. Joan's heart never
burned, but remained untouched amid the ashes, her executioner later testified.

She was rehabilitated in a new trial twenty-five years after
her death, on June 16, 1456, when the French were in complete control of their own country—and Charles VII had no

wish to have his crown rest on the actions of a heretic and sorcerer in league with the Devil. In 1920, she was elevated to sainthood. Today in a square directly opposite the Louvre in Paris, one of the world's most frequently visited museums, there stands a sparkling golden statue of Joan mounted on her horse, wearing full male battle armor.

UNHAPPILY, OVER THE CENTURIES THAT FOLLOWED, inquisitors seeking precedents for conducting witch prosecutions repeatedly cited the cases of Lady Alice and Joan of Arc—the actual court records, as well as second-hand accounts that were brutally unsympathetic to the two women.

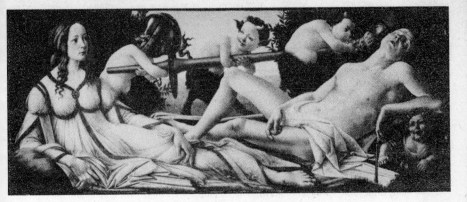

LOVE CONQUERS WAR

In different ways men of the late Middle Ages and Renaissance elaborated the theme of woman as temptress, leading man to his downfall.

For example, fathers passed on to their sons this favorite folktale, with a fabulous cast of characters: Tanhauser, a human minstrel; the goddess Venus; the Virgin Mary; and the Pope:

Hundreds of years ago, a wandering minstrel named Tanhauser was riding through the mountains, singing of his favorite subjects, women and love. All at once, he heard a sweet and lovely call. Looking up he saw the goddess Venus beckoning to him to stay with her in her mountain home. Gladly he went, and for seven years feasted on the delights of love and the senses in the secluded retreat of the goddess. But then, as men will, he grew lonely for the outer world once more. When Venus refused to let him go, he cried out in desperation to the Virgin Mary to come to his aid. Wondrously, a crack appeared in the mountain through which he made his exit. When poor Tanhauser sought absolution for his sins, however, no priest would pardon him. He even went to the Pope himself, but Urban IV (1261–1264) could show him no mercy, saying: "For such blasphemous behavior, for such foul and fleshly misdeeds, it is more likely that this rod in my hand should bloom than that God should grant you pardon."

Tanhauser departed, utterly dejected.

Miraculously, in three days' time the Pope's rod burst into bloom. Urban then sought Tanhauser to pardon him, but all searching was to no avail. Tanhauser had returned to the Mountain of Venus, never again to emerge into the light of day.

Expressing the theme in art, the great painter, Sandro Botticelli (c. 1445–1510) of Florence, portrayed Venus, Roman goddess of love, conquering Mars, Roman god of war—symbolic of woman subduing man. In Botticelli's painting, "Venus and Mars," the goddess is at peace, relaxed and composed. Not a golden hair is out of place. Sitting up, eyes open, she watches the sleeping Mars. Even the playful satyrs surrounding the powerful god cannot awaken him with their games. One delivers a blast on a conch shell, but Mars does not stir. Two other satyrs are making off with his weapons of war, his lance and helmet. —PHOTO COURTESY NATIONAL GALLERY, LONDON

CHAPTER THREE

"The Hammer of Witches"

F inally, with the introduction of the printed page, there was tangible evidence that women were an inferior form of the human species:

What else is a woman but a foe to friendship, an unescapable punishment, a necessary evil, a natural temptation, a desirable calamity, a domestic danger, a delectable detriment, an evil of nature, painted with fair colors!

These words, first written *c.* 390, were scarcely known outside the monastery—until 1486 when they exploded onto the European scene as part of the 250,000-word *Malleus Maleficarum* (Hammer of Witches).* A complete encyclopedia of

---

* The *Malleus* was published and republished at least thirteen times before 1520. There was a long pause while the Reformation held center stage, then between 1574 and 1669, another twenty-one editions were issued. Language barriers, national boundaries, and religious differences proved no obstacle as the text went through thirteen printings in Germany (including the first Protestant edition, at Frankfort in 1580), eleven in France, and two in Italy. Anti-papist England caught up with the Catholic Continent in 1584, ultimately publishing six editions between 1584 and 1669, though there is documentation that two copies were sold at Oxford as early as 1520, and that English intellectuals had read the book long before its British printing.

witchcraft and demonology, the *Malleus* was the handiwork of two enthusiastic Dominican inquisitors, Jakob Sprenger (1436–1495) and his officially appointed associate, Heinrich Kramer (*c.* 1430–1505). Just before compiling their manual —full of every superstition, folktale, and aspersion ever used against woman—the Fathers had tried fifty witches, forty-eight of whom were women.

Authors Sprenger and Kramer had first attracted the attention of the papacy with their hypnotic speeches and inflammatory writings on the subjects of stamping out heresy and promoting the supremacy of the pope. In 1474, Father Sprenger had organized at Cologne the first lay brotherhood devoted to the Rosary. The following year he was made General Inquisitor for all Germany. And five years later, 1480, he became Dean of Cologne University, where his lectures regularly attracted overflow audiences. In the same years, Prior Kramer, head of the Dominican order, traveled far and wide as inquisitor, putting Waldensians to death and rooting out witch societies.

Demonstrating a strong flair for self-promotion, the two Fathers convinced Pope Innocent VIII to issue a papal bull on December 9, 1484, silencing all opponents of witch-hunting— and lending priceless support and publicity to their forthcoming tome.

In his official capacity, the Pope promised "terrible penalties, censures and punishment . . . without any right of appeal" for any who attempt to "molest or hinder . . . Our dear sons Heinrich Kramer and Jakob Sprenger." Throughout Germany, the Fathers were to prosecute "heretical pravaties."

Following the unrestricted endorsement of the Pope, the two inquisitors received full support from Maximilian I, king of Germany and ruler of the Holy Roman Empire, which included much of continental Europe. Maximilian put his official signature on royal letters patent at Brussels on November 6, 1486, and thus gave Fathers Kramer and Sprenger full civil, as well as ecclesiastical, powers in carrying out their inquisitorial duties.

But whereas the Pope had berated men as well as women for the sins of witchcraft, Sprenger and Kramer subtly shifted the emphasis to give women preeminence as witches. In fact, they made the point even for those who never got past the title page, by using the feminine form of the word for witches, *Maleficarum.* (In direct contrast, the more commonly used Latin form, though in the masculine gender, was long accepted as referring to either sex as witch.)

The newness of this emphasis on women comes through in the confusion displayed by Sprenger and Kramer at the beginning of the book. Prescribing the exact methods to extract confession, they constantly refer to "he," "his," and "him," but end by pronouncing most offenders women (italics added for emphasis):

> Witchcraft is high treason against God's Majesty. And so they are to be put to the torture in order to make them confess. Any person, whatever *his* rank or position, upon such an accusation may be put to the torture, and *he* who is found guilty, even if *he* confesses *his* crime, let *him* be racked, let *him* suffer all other tortures prescribed by law in order that *he* may be punished in proportion to *his* offenses.
>
> Note: In days of old, such criminals suffered a double penalty and were often thrown to wild beasts to be devoured by them. Nowadays they are burnt at the stake, and probably this is because *the majority of them are women.*

FOR MORE THAN 200 YEARS, *the Malleus Maleficarum* would serve as a handbook for inquisitors, giving step-by-step instructions on arrest, torture, conviction, and execution of witches.

Fathers Sprenger and Kramer catalogued almost all the reasons used for hunting down witches on both sides of the Atlantic—but buried them beneath a glut of words and endless repetition. Consequently, merciless abridgement of the authors' words and paraphrased headlines of their themes are in order to reveal the stark strength at the core of the book.

Women Predominate Among Witches

It is indeed a fact that it were idle to contradict . . . [that] a greater number of witches is found in the fragile feminine sex than among men.

Jesus Preserved the Superiority of Men

There are more women than men found infected with the heresy of witchcraft. And in consequence of this, it is better called the heresy of witches than of wizards, since the name is taken from the more powerful party. And blessed be the Highest who has so far preserved the male sex from so great a crime: for since He was willing to be born and to suffer for us, therefore He has granted to men this privilege.

Female Weaknesses Include Superstition, Stupidity, and Carnal Lust

There are more superstitious women found than men . . . They are more credulous; and since the chief aim of the Devil is to corrupt faith, therefore he rather attacks them . . .

. . . As regards intellect, or the understanding of spiritual things, they seem to be of a different nature from men, a fact which is vouched for by the logic of the authorities, backed by various examples from the Scriptures. Women are intellectually like children.

. . . All witchcraft comes from carnal lust, which is in women insatiable . . . Wherefore for the sake of fulfilling their lust they consort even with devils.

Heresy is Witchcraft

A woman is by her nature quicker to waver in her faith and consequently quicker to abjure the faith, which is the root of witchcraft.

Female Sexuality is Dangerous

Impurity [is], for example, a woman during her monthly periods.*

We must answer the question why God permits witchcraft to affect the generative powers more than any other human function . . . It is on account of the shamefulness of . . . the venereal act . . . and because the original sin due to the guilt of our first parents is inherited by means of that act.**

---

* This was an ancient tale, born of ignorance and inflamed by superstition. Found in the Old Testament (Leviticus, 15:19), the idea is elaborated by Aristotle (384–322 B.C.), who contends that menstruating women tarnish mirrors, and Pliny the Elder (23–79 A.D.), who warns that a woman who walks through the fields during her period will ruin the crops and wither vines.

** The word "venereal" comes directly from Venus, the goddess of love.

Witchcraft Runs in the Family

Daughters of witches are always suspected of similar practices, as imitators of their mothers' crimes . . . The reason for this . . . is that according to their pact with the Devil, they always have to leave behind them and carefully instruct a survivor, so that they may fulfill their vow to do all they can to increase the number of witches. For how else could it happen, as it has very often been found, that tender girls of eight or ten years have raised up tempests and hailstorms, unless they had been dedicated to the devil under such a pact by their mothers. For the children could not do such things of themselves by abjuring the Faith, which is how all adult witches have to begin, since they have no knowledge of any single article of the Faith.

Beware of Old Women

[Old women are] often inflamed with malice or rage.

Midwives are Wicked Witches

Midwives surpass all others in wickedness.

When [midwives] do not kill the child, they blasphemously offer it to the devil in this manner. As soon as the child is born, the midwife, if the mother is not a witch, carries it out of the room on the pretext of warming it, raises it up, and offers it to the Prince of Devils, that is Lucifer, and to all the devils. And this is done by the kitchen fire.*

---

* At a time when medicine was primitive, these stories would have served to explain stillbirth and infant death. See Chapter One.

Evil Began with Eve

It is true that in the Old Testament, the Scriptures have much that is evil to say about women, and this is because of the first temptress. Eve, and her imitators.

Ancient Writers Recognized Women's Vices

Cicero (106–43 B.C.): "The many lusts of men lead them into one sin, but the one lust of women leads them into all sins: for the root of all woman's vices is avarice."

Seneca (3 B.C.–65 A.D.): "When a woman thinks alone, she thinks evil."

Witches Have a Contract with the Devil

It is a most certain . . . opinion that there are sorcerers and witches who by the help of the Devil, on account of a compact which they have entered into with him are able . . . to produce real and actual evils and harm.

Riding Through the Air at Night
Brings Witches to Faraway Places

We Inquisitors had credible . . . information from a young girl witch who had been converted, whose aunt also had been burned in the diocese of Strasburg. . . . When she was asked whether it was only in imagination and fantastically that they rode, through as illusion of devils, she answered that they did so in both ways.

Women Meet Together in the Nighttime

Certain witches against the instinct of human nature, and indeed against the nature of all beasts with the possible exception of wolves, are in the habit of devouring and eating infant children. And concerning this, the Inquisitor of Como . . . has told us the following: that he was summoned by the inhabitants of the County of Barby to hold an inquisition, because a certain man had missed his child from its cradle, and finding a congress of women in the night-time, swore that he saw them kill his child and drink its blood and devour it.

Witches Cause Storms, Illness,
and Male Impotence

In the diocese of Constance . . . near Salzburg, a violent hailstorm destroyed all the fruit, crops and vineyards in a belt one mile wide, so that the vines hardly bore fruit for three years. This was brought to the notice of the Inquisition, since the people clamoured for an inquiry to be held; many beside all the townsmen being of the opinion that it was caused by witchcraft. Accordingly it was agreed after fifteen days' formal deliberation that it was a case of witchcraft for us to consider; and among a large number of suspects, we particularly examined two women . . . These two were taken and shut up separately in different prisons, neither of them knowing in the least what had happened to the other . . . [Both told exactly the same story] after gentle questioning . . . : They had stirred water into a hole in the name of the Devil and all the devils; and . . . the hailstorm had come after the Devil had taken the water up into the air, and the women returned home. Accordingly, on the third day they were burned.

. . . It is reasonable to conclude that, just as easily as they rail hailstorms, so can they cause lightning and storms at sea; and so no doubt at all remains on these points.

If it is asked how it is possible to distinguish whether an illness is caused by witchcraft or by some natural physical defect, we answer that . . . doctors may perceive from the circumstances, such as the patient's age, healthy complexion, and the reaction of his eyes, that his disease does not result from any defect of the blood or the stomach, or any other infirmity; and they therefore judge that it is not due to any natural defect, but to some extrinsic cause. And since that extrinsic cause cannot be any poisonous infection, which would be accompanied by ill humours in the blood and stomach, they have sufficient reason to judge that it is due to witchcraft. And secondly, when the disease is incurable, so that the patient can be relieved by no drugs, but rather seems to be aggravated by them. Thirdly, the evil may come so suddenly upon a man that it can only be ascribed to witchcraft.

[Some] men are made impotent . . . by witchcraft, . . . and so the contract of marriage is rendered void and matrimony in their cases has become impossible.

Witches can Bewitch their Judges

[They do so] by a mere look or glance from their eyes, and publicly boast that they cannot be punished; and when malefactors have been imprisoned for their crimes, and exposed to the severest torture to make them tell the truth, these witches can endow them with such an obstinacy of preserving silence that they are unable to lay bare their crimes.

A power-mad witch felling a man with her bow and arrow.
From *De Lamiis* (Concerning Witchcraft) by Ulrich Molitor,
1489.—COURTESY HARVARD THEATRE COLLECTION

Never Allow Women to Exercise Power

If we inquire, we find that nearly all the kingdoms of
the world have been overthrown by women . . . The
kingdom of the Romans endured much evil through
Cleopatra, Queen of Egypt, that worst of women. And so
with others. Therefore it is no wonder if the world now
suffers through the malice of women.

Witches can with the help of the Devil bring harm
upon men and their affairs, . . . their reputation, their
body, their reason, and their life.

IN THE *Malleus Maleficarum,* Fathers Kramer and Sprenger fabricated bits of gossip and pieces of hearsay into an Eternal Truth—that evil and femaleness are identical.

The timing of the *Malleus* was remarkable. The book entered the scene in a Europe bewildered and overwhelmed by the turmoil of at least five ongoing revolutions: (1) the Reformation, which pitted established Catholicism against upstarting Protestantism; (2) the replacement of feudal enclaves by national monarchies; (3) the rise of the modern economic system, dominated by commerce and industry; (4) the ascendancy of science, which was demolishing age-old beliefs and superstitions; (5) overseas exploration and empire-building.

None of these revolutions displayed any concern for using the talents of women.

THE RENAISSANCE WITCH

Albrecht Dürer, Germany's greatest artist, was a friend of
Martin Luther, who was leader of the Protestant Reformation
and a staunch believer in witchcraft.

In this picture, titled "Witch, Monster, and Putti," Dürer (1471–1528), portrays a witch riding in the air on a goat, borne aloft by *putti* (boy cupids). Naked, her hair flying wildly in the wind behind her, this witch rides backwards, reflecting the fantasy that witches did everything exactly opposite to the accepted form. She is on her way to or from a sabbath.—PHOTO COURTESY, FOGG MUSEUM OF ART, HARVARD UNIVERSITY

Albrecht Dürer spread witch lore through art; Martin Luther through speeches and writings.

CHAPTER FOUR

"Thou Shalt Not Suffer a Witch to Live"

The *Malleus Maleficarum* had shown the way to get rid of evil, women, witches—all synonymous. Now the Protestants would add their enthusiasm to Catholic determination.

In the midst of turning their backs on the pope, Protestants, starting with Martin Luther in 1517, espoused witchcraft as firmly as did the Catholics—for same reasons and with the same anti-female accusations. In fact, echoing the authors of the *Malleus,* the official Catholic encyclopedia of witchcraft, Luther in 1521 preached:

> Sorcerers or witches are the Devil's whores who steal milk, raise storms, ride on goats or broomsticks, lame or maim people, torture babies in their cradles, change things into different shapes.*

* Luther's friend Albrecht Dürer, Germany's greatest painter and engraver, illustrated these words with inflammatory effect. One example of his engravings on the subject of witchcraft is shown at the front of this chapter.

The single difference between Catholics and Protestants on the subject of witchcraft lay not in the persecution, but in the actual prosecution. The Catholics used ecclesiastic courts, whereas the Protestants relied on civil procedure. The effect was the same.

Like his contemporaries, Martin Luther (1483–1546) had grown up in a household convinced of the evil existence of witches. "That wicked witch, our neighbor, has murdered our poor child," Luther remembered hearing his mother cry when one of his younger brothers died.

A true believer in the evil powers of Satan, Luther advocated the burning of witches even if nothing more could be proved than their making a pact with the Devil. In 1541, he gave express approval to the execution of four witches at Wittenberg.

Similarly, John Calvin (1509–1564), the French-Swiss Protestant leader who gave his name to Calvinism, embraced beliefs current in witchcraft. Preaching to his followers at Geneva, he affirmed: "The Bible teaches us that there are witches and that they must be put to death . . . God expressly commands that all witches and sorceresses must be slain."

Further, he commented: "The fact that the Devil is everywhere called God's adversary, and ours also, ought to fire us to an unceasing struggle against him." In 1545, following a plague epidemic, Calvin urged the authorities at Geneva to take legal action "against witches in order to rid them from the land."

EVEN SO, THE RELIGIOUS REFORMATION, at its beginning, seemed ready to grant women a remission from torture and persecution. And in addition to these negative blessings, there were positive promises of improved status.

For example, both Luther and Calvin worked hard to overthrow the rule of celibacy for priests, and as a result had to praise marriage and woman's role in such a union. In fact, they proved their personal support for the idea that virginity was NOT a higher state than marriage. Both married—though they had been reared and educated as Catholics and were now religious ministers—and thus set an example for their followers.

But this was the sixteenth century and too much radicalism on the question of woman's worth could easily get out of hand. Spontaneously, writings began popping up all over Europe, pillorying and satirizing female foibles. In widely circulated verses both woman and the whole institution of marriage came off badly.

For example, the Continent opined:

> *Two good days for a man in this life—*
> *When he weds and when he buries his wife.*

And in England:

> *When a couple are newly married,*
> *The first month is honeymoon or smick-smack,*
> *The second is hither and thither, the third is thwick-*
> *thwack,*
> *The fourth, the Devil take them that brought thee and*
> *me together.*

Even Luther and Calvin, considered giant reformers by their followers, were content to rest their case by promoting the idea that woman's body was not a sinkhole of sin, that pregnancy and children derived from love. Then they proceeded to put both their own wives, and all women, in their place—well below the husband.

Luther, speaking of his wife, ex-nun Katherine von Bora by whom he had six children after their marriage in 1525, insisted that she had complete control of the household—as long as he retained all his rights. He continued:

> Female government has never done any good. God made Adam master over all creatures, to rule over all living things, but when Eve persuaded him to set himself above God's will, she spoiled everything. 'Tis you women, with your tricks and artifices, that lead men into error.

Frequently, Luther preached that the wife was to be the inferior partner, with her identity completely dependent on her husband's vocation. Her duties as housewife and mother would reach great heights through providing a man with creature comforts, and with children. Luther, whose bed had remained unmade for years prior to his marriage, was quite aware of the advantages of a housekeeping wife.

In an after-dinner conversation recorded by a young disciple, Viet Dietrich of Nuremberg, Luther compared men and women:

> Men have broad shoulders and narrow hips, and more understanding and intelligence than women. Women ought to stay at home, keep house, and bear and bring up children. The way they were created indicates this for they have broad hips and a wide fundament to sit upon.

Likewise, before his marriage in August, 1540—to a widowed Frenchwoman, Idelette de Bure—Calvin had described his notion of the ideal wife to his colleague, the French reformer Guillaume Farel: "a woman who is chaste, agreeable, modest, frugal, patient, and affords me some hope that she will be solicitous for my personal health and prosperity." Apparently, Calvin's wife met these requirements. Following her death after nine years of marriage, he lauded her as never having interfered with his work in any way.

BY THE LATE 1530s Calvinism—which nurtured the Huguenots of France, the Presbyterians of Scotland, and the Puritans of old and New England—had aimed a deadly blow at women. According to Calvin, all that counted in the burgeoning new economic system of trade and industry were the exclusively male virtues of competitiveness, responsibility, and hard work. "Whence do the merchant's profits come, except from his own diligence and industry?" Calvin demanded. And downgrading the importance of land, where the Earth Mother and hence woman had reigned, or at least participated equally, he wrote: "What reason is there why the income from business should not be larger than from landowning?"

In three editions of his *Institution of Christian Religion,* published 1536–1539, Calvin shared with the West his certainty that the male's ability to acquire wealth was all-controlling: "This is granted to the excellence of the male kind: that the children are counted noble or unnoble according to the estate of their father." And Calvin found full support in the Bible for patriarchy: "Oftentimes when the Scripture reckoneth up a genalogie, it nameth the men only. . . . Women are comprehended under the name of men, . . . the name of the household always remaineth with the males."

By way of proving his contentions, Calvin had only to point to the recent revolutionary activities of the Anabaptists. With females conspicuous among them, all Anabaptists dedicated themselves to changing the direction of society. The sect forced both civil and religious officials to abdicate their authority, renounced war, disavowed the pope as well as local bishops, and insisted on the rebaptism of true believers.

So frightened that for once they ignored their own religious differences, Catholics and Lutherans at Speyer, Germany, in 1529 joined in condemning all Anabaptists to death—an order carried out by drowning, burning, decapitation, and hanging.

But this was not the last to be heard from the Anabaptists. In response to the strong measures taken by both Catholic and Protestant authorities, radicals seized control of the sect. Among other actions, these extremists forced men to flee, so that by the time of the major Anabaptists rebellion at Münster in 1534, the population there was about 1700 men, 6800 women, and several thousand children. After a year of turmoil and terrorism, the Roman bishop formerly in charge regained control of Münster and by 1536 executed all Anabaptists leaders, burning the men and burying the women alive. The majority of these martyrs were female.

Obviously there was a lesson crying to be learned here about the need to keep women out of the public arena.

IN THE LATE SIXTEENTH CENTURY and in the seventeenth century newly developed equipment that enabled men to roam the seas or to settle far away in the New World produced a serious surplus of women. Majority status gave no consolation to women.*

Nor did the printing press, constantly being refined and improved, bode well for women. When Johann Gutenberg introduced movable type to Europe some time in the 1450s, his first publication had been the Bible, a beautifully illustrated book the size of a modern-day portable television set. It was impossible to carry around, and equally impossible for anyone not already trained in the fine art of reading manuscripts to decipher easily. The new printing was in well-nigh

---

* In 1576, France's most original and influential political theorist, Jean Bodin, would write of the excessive number of women, which he ascribed to the dangers men alone faced in "war and travel," as well as to the fact that "nature is apter to produce those things that are less perfect."

"Delilah Vanquishes Samson." By Lucas Van Leyden
(1494–1533).—COURTESY FOGG MUSEUM OF ART,
HARVARD UNIVERSITY

illegible type—the letters closely set together in imitation of
the hand-lettering used in manuscripts—and in Latin.

Only with the Reformation did the printing of the Bible in
the vernacular appear. Then the wicked women of the Scriptures became household names, their deeds readily familiar

to all who could read or listen. There was Delilah, who was the ruin of the mighty Samson; Jezebel, who worshipped heathen gods; and of course Eve, who was responsible for all evil since the beginning of time.

By the middle of the sixteenth century, the so-called "Luther's Bible" appeared in German. For women, this Bible was a setback. The approval for extermination of witches was given wider circulation than ever before, now that more men could read and understand the Bible—including the passage from Exodus 22:18: "Die Zauberinnen soltu nicht leben lassen." (Thou shalt not suffer a witch to live.) Whereas previously the Latin had used the neutral *maleficos* to describe evildoers who must not be allowed to live ("Maleficos non patieris vivere."), the German word referred to females alone.

For this same passage, the French-language Bible, *La Saincte Bible,* published at Lyon in 1566, emphasized only the female tradition of evil: "Tu ne laisseras point vivre la sorcière" (female sorceress), and carefully annotated in the margin the reasons for using this word in the feminine gender: "This law applies equally well to men guilty of this crime as to women. But the woman is specified, because this sex by its weakness is more readily deceived by Satan into undertaking such behavior." ("Cette loy a lieu aussi bien aux hommes coulpables de ce crime que aux femmes. Mais il est mention de la femme, à cause de ce sexe par son infirmité est volontiers plustost deçeu par Satan pour s'addonner à cela.)

Similarly, the *Bishops' Bible* published in London, 1568, annotates Exodus 22:17: "Thou shalt not suffer a witche to live. The worde in Hebrew signifieth a witche, a sorcerer, or an inchanter, or any that by suchlike meane hurteth either cattle, corne, or menne."

The *Geneva Bible,* 1560, is particularly significant as the first Bible in English that is divided into verses, the first printed in Roman (modern-day) type, and the first of a size to be carried around comfortably. Again, Exodus 22:18 reads: "Thou shalt not suffre a witche to live."

The unanimity of Continental and English translations, all using the female version of the word, together with the decreased size and increased circulation of the Bible, helped to promote the Great Witch Hunt. Universal Biblical sanction came less than a century after the great encyclopedia *Malleus Maleficarum*.

ADAM AND EVE

God's formula for restoring order out of chaos was stern but simple:

> *The Lord God said to the serpent,*
> *"Because you have done this,*
>   *cursed are you. . . .*
> *. . . To the woman he said,*
>   *"I will greatly multiply your*
>   *pain in childbearing . . . ,*
>   *yet your desire shall be for your husband,*
>   *and he shall rule over you."*

And to Adam he said,
"Because you have listened to the voice
of your wife . . .
cursed is the ground because of you;
in toil you shall eat of it all the
days of your life."

Therefore, the Lord God sent him forth
from the Garden of Eden. . . .
—GENESIS, 3:14–17, 22

Albrecht Dürer's engraving, "Adam and Eve," illustrates the
power of these words. Dürer portrays the couple standing in a
grove of trees, surrounded by many animals, all living together
in complete peace and serenity. Eve is the temptress and Adam is
fast succumbing to her wiles. Showing the female's strong link to
nature, Dürer harks back to another quote from Genesis (3.20):
"And the man called his wife's name Eve, because she was the
mother of all living."

Eve (woman) is responsible for the fall of Adam (man). It
is Eve who accepts the invitation of the serpent, which holds one
of the forbidden fruits in its mouth, offering its delights for the
taking. Only in Adam is tension apparent as he stands, with his
right hand holding onto a branch from another tree, from which
hangs a plaque bearing the artist's name. On the same branch
perches a bird, symbolizing the soul's aspiration toward spiritual
heights. In contrast, the snake must crawl in the mud, dust, and
rock of the earth.

Left-sidedness has long been identified with evil. In fact,
"sinister" is the old Latin word meaning "left." Thus, Adam holds
out his left hand, not his right, for the fruit Eve has plucked from
the forbidden tree.

The proximity of the serpent to Eve in this picture
demonstrates the natural affinity of serpents and women. Both
contain the secret of immortality: the woman reproduces young
from her body and the serpent sheds its skin, becoming young
again each year. Both echo in their own bodies the keys to life:

birth and death, the change of seasons, the cyclical nature of human existence.—PICTURE COURTESY MUSEUM OF FINE ARTS, BOSTON

The Bible, literature, and art all pointed to masculine rule, feminine subordination—by force if necessary.

CHAPTER FIVE

"Woman Should Be Subject"

The natural calamities of famine and plague, combined with man-made political and economic disasters and radical changes in society finally brought about the Great Witch Hunt. It accelerated in central Europe around 1550, and petered out across the ocean in Salem, Massachusetts, after 1692. Hundreds of thousands, maybe millions, were marched to the stake or forced to the gallows. Executions, almost always in groups, numbered five or six women for every one man.

Switzerland furnishes an excellent case study for the first fifty or so years of the Hunt. Located in the heart of Western Europe, at the crossroads between the Protestant Reformation and the Catholic Counter-Reformation, the area was also the longtime home for the Waldensian heretics, whose very name had been synonymous with witchcraft since around 1450. These were the legendary Waldensians who flew by night to the sabbath with the Devil, where they performed their black magic.

There is at least one specific indication in the records of witchcraft at Geneva that accusations were first directed at men and women alike, then almost exclusively at women. When a mild epidemic of plague broke out, 1542–1545, husbands as well as wives confessed to preparing and spreading the germs, a technique they reported learning from the

Devil. By 1571, however, when the worst panic about plague-spreaders occurred, ninety-one out of ninety-nine of those identified as witch-agents of the Devil were women.

Of these ninety-one women, forty-five were widows, thirty-two were actively married, and fourteen unmarried. Significantly, almost all were past forty, meaning that they could no longer bear children, yet they still required food, shelter, and clothing. Unable to support themselves in any other way, such women often claimed powers to cure animals, children, spouses, parents, anyone, in return for bare sustenance.

Nor did anyone question such claims. It was long-accepted wisdom that women who toiled in the fields or who lived in the woods knew all about plants for food and herbs for medicine. Described repeatedly as knowing how to use herbs to heal or to harm, women no doubt experimented. In other words, a woman might cure an illness by skill or by luck, and gain a good reputation and a new source of income. Conversely, in an atmosphere already thick with superstition, chance or ignorance might make her fail so that eventually she could scare enemies to death just by cursing them verbally or hexing them by sticking pins in their image.

For example, at Neuchatel in northwest Switzerland, Clauda Brunye, a forty-year-old wanderer, was arrested for failing to cure a woman possessed by the Devil (i.e., seriously ill, mentally or physically). Tortured, Clauda confessed that her own personal devil was Cajy, a familiar (demonic servant in the form of an insect or an animal) whom she carried with her always in a small container. Cajy, she said, gave her instructions on both causing and curing illness and stirring hail storms by dancing naked on hilltops. All these things she did regularly together with other witches whom she obligingly named. Some of the group's greatest feats included killing the husband of a client in less than six days by poisoning his soup and bringing death by plague to four humans and herds of cattle. Once, just to show off, they had bewitched a peasant's cart into halting completely in the middle of the road. Clauda was burned alive, September 16, 1568.

Records from Neuchatel are often quoted, since they are remarkably complete, containing even small details that heighten the horror of execution. They describe how church bells tolled during the sentencing and the final burning on the pyre—adding that sometimes the bells were covered with wet cloth to insure a more mournful pealing. The accused witch is pictured kneeling before spectators to recite the summary of her trial and to certify the justice of the sentence. (This universal practice helped to spread the same or similar accusations and confessions, couched in near-identical words, everywhere.) If she refused, she would be sent back to prison for further torture. Her execution would be a public spectacle, proclaimed by blaring trumpets and those ringing bells—with even children having the day off from school to attend—to insure that everyone understood the fate of witches and could see for themselves the cleansing of society. Following the execution, anyone with names of additional suspects was invited to come forth.

A prototype of most witch trials was that of Jehanne Berna at Neuchatel, January 5, 1583. First of all, she was an outsider who came not from Neuchatel but from the nearby Duchy of Savoy. In addition, she was a widow with a strong personality, accused of having acted as leader in an assembly several weeks before, where many women were seen dancing around a fire. And under torture, before her sentence of being burned alive was carried out, she named three additional women as accomplices.

One accomplice, Perrenon Debrot, was also an outsider who pictured herself as "all alone in the world." She was arrested on January 16, together with Elise le Royer of Morat, also named by Jehanne Berna. Tortured, they both added further details to the description of the sabbath: "It was held from 10 to

11 P.M. one Saturday night, and there was dancing in the street, lighted by blue candles held by Jehanne."

The third accomplice, Marie Breguet, was an outsider from the Pays de Vaud and also a widow. As had the others, she described the sabbath, gave the inquisitors still more names, and then went further, embellishing the story of the sabbath with tales of herbs received from the Devil "to make grease to rub on windows and door knobs so that people would die when they touched it."

In a second round of arrests, Antonia Preudhon defied all superstition and earthly authority by strangling herself before the arrival of the executioner—who, to make certain her soul could harm no one, dragged the corpse through the city of Neuchatel and then threw the body on the fire already consuming her co-conspirator Madeleine Merlou. A fellow prisoner, Perrenon Gerard, somehow escaped from jail and attempted to commit suicide with a knife when recaptured. She was put to death a week later on February 22. In the end, eight were executed and one committed suicide in this Neuchatel witch-hunt of 1583. All were women, all were named by others similarly accused, all repeated the story of the sabbath with the Devil, including the candles colored blue and the plague-spreading grease rubbed on doorknobs and locks.

At least, Antonia Preudhon by suicide and Perrenon Gerard by attempting to kill herself managed to send direct messages to posterity—unchanged and uncensored by official recorders. The actual records of testimony and confession tell something about the persecutor and prosecutor but nothing about the accused witches themselves—what they believed, the kind of lives they led, their relationships with family, neighbors, and other human beings. All words come filtered through the authorities, censored (as shown in the case of Joan of Arc) with key sections illegible or lost completely. The accused thus became a wooden stereotype against which the judge or prosecutor hurled leading questions that already contained the an-

swer: "How long have you been in the service of the Devil?"
instead of the direct and simple, "Are you in fact in the service
of the Devil?"

The women accused as witches almost never wrote about
themselves. They had little education and so were unable to
express themselves on paper. On the other hand, women-
witches were the objects of countless manuscripts and books
by inquisitors, tract writers, theologians, and eyewitnesses. In
their eyes even the supreme rebelliousness expressed by an
accused witch in taking or attempting to take her own life
could be distorted into an act inspired by the Devil. For example, here is the comment made by Henri Boguet, fifty-
three-year-old lawyer and witchcraft judge of Burgundy
(southeastern France, not far from Switzerland), writing his
much admired tract *Treatise on Witches* (*Discours des Sor-
ciers*):

> Witches have strangled themselves, it seems, at the
> instigation of Satan. For, fearing lest witches, in dying at
> the hands of Justice should be induced to repent, he either
> kills them or impels them to kill themselves, so that they
> may not escape him.

IN A KIND OF SEESAW EFFECT, history began putting more
and more outspoken women to death as witches in the sixteenth century and at the same time gave females their last
real chance to exercise meaningful power. Spain had Isabella
and Ferdinand in charge as joint monarchs at the turn of the
century; for fifty years, 1553–1603, England was ruled by
queens, first Mary, 1553–1558, then Elizabeth the Great; in
Scotland the French-born regent, Mary of Guise, held power
sometime after the death of her husband, James V, in 1542,
until the accession of her daughter Mary Queen of Scots, in
1561; and France (temporarily closing its eyes to the 1317
edict prohibiting women from exercising rule) was controlled

by Queen-regent Catherine de Medici from 1558 to around 1574.

But this was the final death rattle of power for women. Looking at these queens, John Knox, a forty-five-year-old refugee from Scotland where he had led the Reformation, set himself up as spokesman for the commonly believed wisdom of the day, that women had no talent for ruling. His printed outburst—first published anonymously—started making the rounds of the Continent and Britain late in 1558, titled *The First Blast of the Trumpet against the Monstrous Regiment of Women*. Written in Geneva while he worked closely with Calvin, nastiness followed insult in an attempt to eradicate queenship forever:

> To promote a woman to bear rule, superiority, dominion, or empire above any realm, nation or city is repugnant to Nature, contumely to God, a thing most contrary to His revealed will and approved ordinance; and finally it is the subversion of good order, of all equity and justice . . . For who can deny but it is repugnant to Nature that the blind shall be appointed to lead and conduct those as do see? That the weak, sick and impotent persons shall nourish and keep the whole strong? And finally that the foolish, mad and phrenetic shall govern the discreet and give counsel to such as be of sober mind? And such be all women, compared unto men in bearing of authority . . . Woman in her greatest perfection was made to serve and obey man, not to rule and command him . . .

This bitter man, forced out of Scotland by the Catholic Queen-regent, Mary of Guise, was equally hounded in the England of Mary Tudor (1553-1558), known to history as Bloody Mary for her attempt by killing and massacre to turn England back from its newly acquired Protestantism to

Catholicism. But his timing was terrible. His tract made its appearance in England simultaneously with the coronation of Queen Elizabeth, darling of the Protestants and a monarch adored by her people.

Halfheartedly, Calvin himself moved to appease the anger of Queen Elizabeth, writing to her chief adviser and Lord Treasurer, Sir William Cecil, in 1559:

> John Knox asked of me in private conversation what I thought about the Government of Women. I candidly replied that, as it was a deviation from the original and proper order of nature, it was to be ranked, no less than slavery, among the punishments consequent upon the fall of man, but that there occasionally were women so endowed that it was evident that they were "raised up" by Divine authority.

MORE AND MORE, as wealth rather than mere subsistence became life's goal, man went into the outer world, leaving behind at home the wife he characterized as physically weak and intellectually incapable. It followed naturally that government was to be exercised by men only, and any woman questioning the God-given system was a witch who was to be treated, punished, and executed as such—to purge society of evil as well as to set an example for others of like mind. By 1575, Jean Bodin of France, a forty-six-year-old lawyer and professor, assumed the mantle of spokesman for these views.

The case that converted Bodin into a true believer was one that he heard himself, sitting as a trial judge in April, 1578, that of Jeanne Harvellier of Verbery. "Without being tortured," he wrote, "she described her thirty-eight year love affair with the Devil," who regularly visited her. She pictured Satan as "a large black man, much bigger than ordinary men, dressed in black." Sometimes he came to her on horseback at night, and at other times she went on a long, exhausting journey to a sabbath where the revels occurred and where she participated in the killing of men and beasts.

Bodin minces no words insisting that punishment and/or death for witchcraft will frighten potential evil-doers back into submission. Despite his reputation as a scholar and lawyer, he thinks the law should be bent or even ignored totally to purge society in order to maintain the health and greatness of the state:

> The country which shall [let witches escape] will be scourged with pestilences, famines, and wars. . . . One accused of being a witch ought never to be fully acquitted and set free . . . , inasmuch as the proof of such crimes is so obscure and so difficult that not one witch in a million would be accused or punished if the procedure were governed by the ordinary rules.

His masterpiece, *Six Books of the Commonwealth,* is spattered with disdain for women daring to exercise authority:

> The rule and government of women is directly against the law of nature, which hath given unto men wisdom, strength, courage, and power to command; and taken the same from women. Yea the law of God hath expressly ordained that the woman should be subject unto the man, and that not only in the government of kingdoms and empires, but also in every particular man's house and family. To make women mistresses over men is of all miseries and calamities the worst.

Not in the least surprisingly, Bodin's next tract was *Demonmanie des Sorcières,* Demon-madness of Witches, which went through fifteen editions in four languages between 1580 and 1605 to become his second most popular book.

European painting also reflected the attitudes of society toward women and evil. For example, the French Jean Cousin (c. 1490–1560) painted a voluptuous Eve lying nearly naked in a dark woodland grotto, surrounded on every side with sinister objects. Adam is nowhere to be seen. For any viewer who might miss the point, the artist has emblazoned at the top of the picture a sign reading "EVA PRIMA PANDORA." In Greek mythology the equally beautiful, equally treacherous Pandora was the first woman sent to earth by Zeus, king of the gods. Her mission was to punish the human race for stealing fire from heaven. She carried with her a vase (often and mistakenly called a box), containing all human ills as well as hope. Uncovering the vase allowed evil to escape. Eve's hand only partially covers the top of the vase beside her.—COURTESY LOUVRE MUSEUM, PARIS

Unhappily for women, Bodin's lofty reputation made him a formidable literary leader who almost single-handedly provided a scholarly basis for witch hunting. And Bodin was convinced that women were the witches:

Ordinarily women rather than men are demoniacal, and by diabolical means witches are often transported in body and often put in an ecstatic state with the soul separate from the body and the body remaining senseless and dumb.

LILITH
AND THE MONSTERS
OF THE NIGHT

The infamous female monster Lilith—called the queen of the *succubi* (female demons)—appears here in the form by which she was most often symbolized in Europe, the nocturnal, predatory owl.

Perched on a human skull amidst the crumbling ruins of an ancient tomb, Lilith senses her enemy, the sun, rising brilliantly behind her, compelling her to return to her sinister abode in the woods. The motto written in Middle German beside the owl reads "Ich Fyrcht Den Tag" or "I Dread The Day."

—COURTESY FOGG ART MUSEUM, HARVARD UNIVERSITY

THE OWL

Typical of the terrifying tales told of Lilith in her guise as an owl was this one, finally written down by the Brothers Grimm in the nineteenth century:

Many hundreds of years ago a horned monster lost its way. It was an owl with sharp talons and two tall, feathery horns, one above each eye. Spotting an open barn door, in a quiet little village located on the edge of a deep, dark forest, the creature flew inside and perched on a rafter to spend the night.

Bright and early the next morning the farmer came in to milk the cows. But catching sight of the monster, he raced outside, terrified. He screamed to his neighbors for help. They all came running, armed with pitchforks and scythes. One look at those huge, foreboding eyes, however, froze them in their tracks.

So the farmer sent for the man known as the bravest and strongest in the entire village. "Have courage," the fearless one assured them. "It will not stare at us much longer!" And he pranced into the barn as if he were going to gather the morning eggs, sitting primly in their little nests.

But he saw those eyes big as saucers and just as unwavering, those feathered horns rising under the monster's head like the horns of some demon from the underworld.

The rescuer reached no further than the fifth rung of the ladder. He half-slid, half-fell to the ground and sped out of the barn.

The villagers were in a frenzy. Their best man had just run away. The creature threatened to destroy them all. Finally, the town burgomaster proposed that everyone contribute enough money to pay the owner for his barn and all his hay, corn, and animals inside.

The next morning, where the barn had once stood, nothing but grey ashes remained.

And the owl was no more.—ADAPTED FROM GRIMM #174

No book on witchcraft is complete without Lilith, Adam's defiant first wife. But any historian who omits her deserves sympathy, not a scolding.

First of all, her story and description are full of confusing contradictions. Either she was history's first feminist, demanding full equality with her husband, deserting when this was denied—or she was a night monster, preying on sleeping men, terrorizing women in pregnancy, strangling helpless infants before they had even been named.

Second, she crops up in very early literature—in the Book of Isaiah in the Old Testament, for example, circa 700 B.C.—only to disappear for centuries at a time, re-emerging in the sixth century A.D., returning some seven centuries later in the waning Middle Ages, and making final appearances in the seventeenth century.

Third, she is hard to find, frequently hidden under other names—as in the 1611 King James version of the Bible which in Isaiah 34:14 uses the words "screech owl" for the original Hebrew "Lilith." And throughout the Salem records there are repeated references to attacks by Lilith and her retinue of female demons, the *succubi,* without ever mentioning Lilith by name.

THE FIRST RECORDED LEGEND of the creation of Lilith—in a sixth century A.D. book of Judaism brought in from the East, *The Alphabet of Ben Sira*—excites modern feminists:

> . . . To banish his loneliness, Lilith was first given to Adam as wife. Like him she had been created out of the dust of the ground ["adamah" in Hebrew, a feminine word for "earth" or "soil"]. But she remained with him only a short time, because she insisted upon enjoying full equality with her husband. She derived her rights from their identical origin. . . . Lilith flew away from Adam, and vanished in the air. Adam complained before God that the wife He had given him had deserted him, and God sent forth three angels to capture her. They found her in the Red Sea, and they sought to make her go back with the threat that, unless she went, she would lose a hundred of her demon children daily by death. But Lilith preferred this punishment to living with Adam. . . .

But then the story concludes with the contradiction non-violent feminists find hard to swallow:

> She takes her revenge by injuring babies—baby boys during the first night of their life, while baby girls are exposed to her wicked designs until they are twenty days old. . . .*

THE TALE OF LILITH began spinning its way into Western consciousness around the thirteenth century when it was

* This translation is taken from the most readily available source, Louis Ginzberg's *Legends of the Jews,* first published in 1912.

eagerly assimilated into the education of French intellectuals. The Zohar, or Book of Splendor, asserted that Lilith's powers were at their height when the moon was on the wane. During these hours of increasing darkness at night, demons and evil spirits took control.

In a description startlingly reminiscent of the witches' sabbath in medieval Christian demonology, the Zohar—the basic work of the Kabbalah, the collected writings of Jewish mysticism based on the Bible—portrays Lilith along with her other succubi, Naaman, Agrath, and Mahalath. They "gather on a particular mountain near the mountains of darkness" where they frolic with Samael, the demon lover Lilith took after Adam. (The name "Samael" means "left," synonymous in the Middle Ages with "sinister.")

A seventeenth century witchcraft tract writer, Peter de Loier, explained that as a Frenchman he had learned of Lilith from "the Jews who for a long time were abiding in France, and out of their Caball." De Loier then proceeds to describe Lilith and her retinue of succubi in his *Treatise of Specters,* translated from French into English in 1605:

> Succubi which are devils . . . taking the form of women, do seek to enjoy their pleasure of men. Of which succubi the chief princess or commandress is called by the rabbis, Lilith: That is to say, an apparition of the night, from the name Laila, which signifieth night. For such devils do not use or exercise their force against men but in the night-time.

Shrewdly, De Loier dedicated his book to King James of Great Britain, a true believer in witchcraft, thus helping to promote its circulation in England.

And sure enough, by the late seventeenth century, John Webster, a leading English physician though generally skeptical on the subject of witchcraft, described the horrible activities of Lilith. He referred to her by name in his treatise, *The Displaying of Supposed Witchcraft,* 1677, but likened her to an owl:

> Lilith . . . is taken to be a kind of owl, . . . blind upon the day, and flying abroad upon the nights, making an horrible noise, and were to be found about Rome, Helvetia, and Crete or Candy, and do certainly suck the dugs of goats, that thereby they waste away and become blind. And that they are also sometimes found in Denmark, that learned physician and laborious anatomist Bartholinus doth make manifest, and that they do suck the breasts or navels of young children.

Significantly, this treatise turned up in the late seventeenth century libraries of Harvard President Increase Mather and his brilliant son, Cotton.

BY THE PERIOD of the Great Witch Hunt, then, woman who had once basked in the reflected glory of the Earth Mother was tainted by sharing the sex of Lilith.

· Part II ·

WITCH HUNTING
IN BRITAIN

"THE WITCHES' KITCHEN"

In this painting by Frans Francken II (1581–1642) there are
women of all ages and all walks of life. Noblewomen, conspicuous

for their stylish clothes, are present along with peasants,
demonstrating that witchcraft cut across social and economic lines,
but was dominated by a single sex. The only male figure is the
grotesquely severed, one-eyed head of a warrior on the floor in the
lower right-hand corner.

Every possible tool and ingredient required by the witches is crammed into this scene: snakes, skulls, frogs, turtles, toads, cats, and bats. Also, there are books of spells, a satanic goat, and secret ointment. In the lower left, a group of women bow down to a demonic figure which stands on an altar, an obvious parody of the Mass. And just above this, the naked backside of a witch soars up the chimney on a broomstick.

A witch standing in the center stirs her goat's head brew with a broom. The kitchen, the hearth, the broom—these are all symbols of the home, used here by witches.

The noble ladies make ready to strip off all their clothes, so that an old witch can rub their bodies with the magic ointment. Then they will each board brooms and fly through the night. The artist has even included a view of a church just outside this blasphemous kitchen. It appears dark and foreboding, almost abandoned in its bleakness.

This painting is a visual composite of all the witchcraft testimony circulating in Europe. There is not a grain of evidence that such a scene as this ever did exist.—PICTURE COURTESY KUNSTHISTORISCHEN MUSEUM, VIENNA

CHAPTER SIX

"The Discoverie of Witchcraft"

The sabbath. Flying through the air on poles or broomsticks. Animals as familiars. Pact with the devil. Witch's marks. Magical ointment.

In bits and snatches the vocabulary and paraphernalia of witch lore came to Great Britain by the second half of the sixteenth century. And tales spread far and wide as the more sensational trials for witchcraft were reported immediately in a blackletter broadside, which in those days of no newspapers took the place of a scandal sheet. One of the first was *The Examination and Confession of Certain Witches at Chelmsford* (England), published 1566.

The Chelmsford trial in Essex County introduced into English consciousness three solid precedents for seventeenth century witch-hunts in old and New England: (1) discovery of witch's marks on the body of the accused, from which the Devil could suck his quota of blood; (2) a familiar (personal, always-available demon) in the form of a cat; (3) evidence based almost wholly on the testimony of a child, in this case a twelve-year-old girl named Agnes Brown.

The three defendants were a sixty-three-year-old widow, Agnes "Mother" Waterhouse, her eighteen-year-old daughter Joan, and Elizabeth Francis who became involved by giving her white, spotted, old (fifteen years) cat, fittingly named Sathan, to Mother Waterhouse.

As Elizabeth Francis had promised, Sathan carried out all of Mother Waterhouse's commands: killing a neighbor, William Fynee, as well as husband Waterhouse; and destroying neighbors' pigs, cows, and geese. In return Mother Waterhouse allowed Sathan to suck blood from her hands or face. And from time to time she turned Sathan into a toad—the incarnation of evil according to superstition. The one defeat suffered by the cat and witch was failing to murder another neighbor named Wardol because, according to the trial record, "he was so strong in faith that Sathan had no power to hurt him."

Born in the years when England was still Catholic, old Mother Waterhouse admitted saying her prayers in Latin instead of English. This was at the time of intense plotting by

A witch and her cat. From a seventeenth century English chapbook.—COURTESY BRITISH LIBRARY

Catholic Mary Queen of Scots against England's Queen
Elizabeth. The County government saw the hand of the Devil
everywhere, and so delegated four of its most respected judges
to hear the case: Thomas Cole, rector of Stanford Rivers,
located ten miles from Chelmsford, probably to protect the
claims of the royal Church against Catholicism; Sir John
Fortescue, who would soon become Chancellor of the Ex-
chequer; Sir Gilbert Gerard, the Queen's Attorney; and John
Southcote, justice of the Queen's Bench. Thus the trial was a
clash between judges who were highly respected men and
defendants who were wretched women. The prestige of the
judges set precedents followed all through the seventeenth
century in every English-speaking witch trial.

Mother Waterhouse as a Catholic and thus an outsider, and
also an old woman—by current definition a useless burden to
society—was excellent fodder for the gallows. She was found
guilty on July 27, 1566 and hanged two days later.

Joan Waterhouse turned state's evidence against her mother
and so was released. The court found Elizabeth Francis guilty
of the lesser crime of bewitching, and under the law recently
enacted by Queen Elizabeth, in 1563, sentenced her to one year
in prison. But she refused to be suppressed, and after leaving
prison was again convicted of bewitching and imprisoned for
another year. Released, she took almost ten years to get into
trouble again, and in 1579 went on trial at Chelmsford with
three other women, all half-starved beggars (true of many
accused as witches). Elizabeth Francis and two of the other
women were convicted and hanged. But in the case of the
fourth woman, Margery Stanton, the judges deemed the evidence insufficient—without further explanation—and so set
her free.

At the time, it was accepted without question that a mother-
witch would spawn a daughter-witch—in order to pass the
secrets of witchcraft on from one generation to the next. Thus
in this case, Ellen Smith, one of three who were hanged in

1579 was the daughter of a woman executed in 1574 as a witch. Ellen was accused of bewitching a four-year-old child. This would have been a minor offense, except that the child had died just after screaming, "Away with the witch." In addition, the child's mother, Goodwife Webbe, was reported to have gone out of her mind forever when she saw a familiar, this time in the form of a black dog, leave the room immediately after the death.

FURTHER NORTH IN THE SAME DECADE, Scotland arrested Bessie Dunlop for witchcraft. Once again, a Catholic outsider, a woman, went on trial for her life before Protestant judges.

Remarkably, a new kind of character appears in this case, playing a prime role—a ghost. Alive some thirty years before as Thom Reid, he had gone off to war and was slaughtered on the battlefield at Pinkie, where Henry VIII of England fought to add Scotland to his royal domains. Even as a ghost, Thom's reappearance was a strong reminder that the newly powerful Protestant nobility faced constant subversion from local Catholics.

The court accused Bessie of acting as the ghost's living agent, specially trained to carry out his orders to destroy. She had come to the judges' attention when as midwife she failed to deliver healthy infants, and as herbalist her treatment of sick people resulted in death.

Rare among females accused as witches, Bessie emerges as a very human, painfully troubled woman—thanks to the meticulous research of Robert Pitcairn who in 1833 compiled the four-volume *Criminal Trials in Scotland . . . 1488–1624.* Thus Bessie's description of her first meeting with the Devil portrays her venturing forth in a daze to do an errand, weeping from pain in the aftermath of childbirth, terrified that her child and sick husband were both about to die. The court report included—and Pitcairn emphasized—her explanation how it happened that the ghost of a local wizard, Thom Reid, that staunch Catholic, came to teach her witchcraft:

> As she was going between her own house and the yard of Monkcastell [the estate where she and her husband lived as tenants], driving her cow to the pasture and making heavy fair dole with herself, grieving very hard for her cow that was dead, her husband and child that were lying sick in the land ill, and she new rising out of gissane [childbirth from the old French "gisante," a woman lying in the straw], the aforesaid Thom met her by the way, hailed her, and said, "Good day, Bessie," and she said, "God speed you goodman."

Then under prompting by the judges, and leading questions, Bessie told a story that fitted in perfectly with local lore. Thom Reid took her to a witches' coven, she testified, where eight elegant ladies and four knights were meeting and where she received curative herbs from the Queen of the Fairies. Thom Reid then taught her professional midwifery and cures for all illnesses. But later, Bessie's silence when the twelve invited her to go away with them made them all disappear in a blast of wind. The ghost who had remained hidden during the interview reappeared, explaining that Bessie had rejected twelve fairies from the Elfin Court. Bessie still refused to speak and, though annoyed, the ghost continued to help her.*

The case of Bessie Dunlop provided important paraphernalia for the future because it introduced the witches' coven or sabbath to Britain—though in the form of a simple meeting,

---

* Paraphrase rather than direct quote has been used to tell this second part of the story. Here, Pitcairn has copied down the testimony with all its endlessly repetitive detail and almost unreadable sixteenth century Scots-English.

which would soon be embellished with wild Continental additions.

The kind of torture used to produce her testimony—quite similar to that used as late as 1692 in Salem, Massachusetts—was carefully described by Pitcairn in the introduction to her case:

Solitary confinement, cold and famine, extreme thirst, the want of sleep and the privation of all the comforts, even the commonest necessaries of life, the desertion of their affrighted relations and friends, added to the cruelest tortures, generally induced them at length, weary of life, to make their "confession" as it was called . . . Even the indulgence of lying in a reclining posture on their hand-ful of straw was frequently denied them . . . Day and night "waked" and watched by some skillful person ap-pointed by her inquisitors, the unhappy creature, after a few days of such discipline, maddened by the misery of her forlorn and helpless state, would be rendered fit for "confessing" anything, in order to be rid of the dregs of her wretched life. At intervals, fresh examinations took place, and these were repeated from time to time, until her "contumacy," as it was termed, was subdued . . . Trials followed closely on the emission of one or more of the Declarations or Confessions thus obtained, which formed the groundwork of the public accusation and prosecution. The [Court] having merely to compare the indictment . . . with the previously extorted Confession and other such written or oral testimony as the prosecutor chose to adduce, returned their verdict . . . Doom was, of course, pronounced in terms of law—and in a few hours the wretched victim was led out to the stake, to be strangled and burnt to ashes.

Parenthetically, one difference between Scotland and England should be noted here. The English—and their American colonists—regarded burning at the stake barbaric, and so executed their witches by hanging them. The executioner gently "turned them off." In other words, he would remove the step or ladder on which the convicted witch stood, so that the noose around the neck was the body's only support. "Hanging by the neck till dead" meant instant execution.

BESSIE DUNLOP was "burnt to ashes" on November 8, 1576. Not quite five years later, the French political scientist and demonologist, Jean Bodin, crossed the English Channel to make himself and his views seen and heard in Britain.

Bodin and his writings provoked a detailed rebuttal from Reginald Scot, a forty-six-year-old country gentleman. A former student at Oxford who had served in Parliament for one year, Scot wrote *The Discoverie of Witchcraft* in 1584.

A sly sense of humor shines through Scot's writing, especially in comparison to all the other witchcraft tracts, which are deadly serious and woman-hating. For example, he soberly knocks down the cliché-worn superstition that witches can prevent the forming of butter from cream, by adding mockingly, "especially if either the maids have eaten up the cream, or the goodwife has sold the butter before in the market." Then he goes on to advise sarcastically: "Put a little soap or sugar into your churn of cream, and there will never come any butter, churn as long as you like."

Again, referring to the common description of the old, flying witch, he taunts: "What an unapt instrument is a toothless, old, impotent, and unwieldy woman to fly in the air? Truly, the Devil little needs such instruments to bring his purposes to pass."

He pities such women as starving beggars going from door to door for food, "without the which they could hardly live."

And he accuses of outright ignorance anyone who blames illness and adversity on witchcraft.

Referring to the often repeated popular tale, recently brought in from the Continent, that witches could rub themselves with a special ointment and then fly through the air to accomplish great magical feats, Scot proclaims triumphantly that the carefully witnessed results of using such ointment "greatly overthroweth the opinion of *Malleus Maleficarum,* Bodin, and such others as write so absolutely in maintenance of witches' transportation." Scot tells the story of an old witch who rubs herself all over with ointment and falls into a "most sound and heavy sleep." Even when her observers beat her fiercely, she had no sense of feeling. Eventually the effects of the ointment wore off and she told stories of flying over "both seas and mountains, delivering to us many untrue and false reports. We earnestly denied them, she impudently affirmed them."

On another subject, turning from gentle criticism to harsh logic, he sympathizes with women in menopause who become melancholy and so turn to what he labels "fantasies."

Scot finds that melancholy has such incredible effects on some women that they imagine that "they are . . . monarchs and princes and that all other men are their subjects."

Scot's playful reference here to feminist aspirations was completely in tune with the temper of the times, when Queen Elizabeth's subjects, and indeed all of Europe, considered her the West's most effective and powerful monarch. Nor did Elizabeth, holding the reins of government, worry that female witches might gain control of the nation by using that diabolical Continental device, a pact with the Devil.

Queen Elizabeth refused to promote an intensive witch-hunt, despite the stories of witch plots against her life or witch fortune-tellers claiming to know when she would die (thus provoking chaos or rebellion).

For every skeptical Reginald Scot of England, however,

there were at least twelve tract writers who equated witchcraft with female evil—hardly the kind of argument that would appeal to Elizabeth. Thus she asked Parliament to enact only a relatively mild law against witchcraft in 1563, at the start of her reign—the statute under which such sporadic trials as those of the witches of Chelmsford occurred. Later, in 1580, she had Parliament pass "An Act against seditious words and rumours uttered against the Queen's most excellent Majesty" —reflecting her greater interest in tracking down threatening enemies rather than pursuing witches.

BUT THIS LIGHT-HEARTED ATTITUDE toward witchcraft—reflected in Scot, as well as most of the late sixteenth century English literature—began to disappear as the century came to a close. England was thrown into a state of frightening confusion as Elizabeth aged toward death and showed signs of unaccustomed senility. Lurking in the background were two possible successors, each terrifyingly unthinkable. Stronger and most likely was Elizabeth's cousin, James VI of Scotland. Wonder of wonders, he was the Protestant son of Catholic Mary Queen of Scots, whom Elizabeth had executed in 1587 as a threat to England in general and to Elizabeth personally. The other possibility was even worse: a woman, Arabella Stuart, with strong Catholic support, even including the Pope at Rome.

An immediate reflection of this charged emotional climate was the changed attitude of writers. Even Edmund Spenser (1552–1599), whose long allegorical poem *The Faerie Queene* dealt with Glory in the abstract and the magnificence of his Queen, Elizabeth, in particular, could not resist painting pictures of women as evil threats to men.

Thus in Book III of the allegory he portrays the most complete witch in English tradition:

FOR WOMEN ONLY

The painting "Diana and Actaeon" depicts the moment when Diana caught the mortal hunter spying on her. Diana is shown naked at her bath, a tiny crescent moon adorning her forehead. Her glorious handmaidens are attempting to shield her from view.

When Actaeon intruded, however unknowingly, on her privacy, Diana used her magical powers to change him into prey for his own previously faithful hounds. He would never be able to tell the world that he had seen the goddess in her nakedness, or reveal her most sacred mysteries—including how to protect women in childbirth and how to assist midwives in delivery.

In the painting, Actaeon still has the body of a man, but his head has turned dark and furry, with antlers sprouting from it. The helpless hunter, with artist's license, can be seen simultaneously in the dim background, lying on his back, four

spindly legs raised in the air, being consumed by his own dogs.
ECOLE DE FONTAINEBLEAU, XVI C. LOUVRE MUSEUM, PARIS

To men, the ways of the goddess Diana and, by association, the ways of women—similarly reputed to meet at night in the woods, stripped naked for the witches' sabbath—seem horrifyingly demonic and inscrutable.

CHAPTER SEVEN

"Daemonologie"

James VI of Scotland was a devoted scholar who read and spoke five languages, and wrote long treatises on every subject imaginable—from the evils of tobacco and the dangers of witches to the need for peace among nations. But he was a mental mess.

His accession to the throne of Scotland in 1587 marked the end of a miserable adolescence. In 1567, at the age of one year, he had been abandoned forever by his mother, Mary Queen of Scots, and had lost his father Lord Darnley to murder (by his mother and her lover, the strong rumor hinted). He himself had constantly been kidnapped by bands of roving nobles and returned at their convenience.

The moment Elizabeth of England put his mother to death in 1587, she began dangling the English kingship before James. But his painful wait for the great prize of mighty England and his extraordinary care to ingratiate himself with Queen Bess took a seemingly endless sixteen years. It was not until March 24, 1603, at around two o'clock in the morning that the dying, seventy-year-old queen mumbled something about her successor that those around her translated as "Who should that be but our cousin of Scotland?"

During this sixteen-year-wait, 1587–1603, small wonder that James who had made a special study of Continental witchcraft was forever seeing bad omens and espying old women using their evil crafts to try to kill him.

In fact, no sooner had James come to Scotland's throne in the late 1580s than he found himself exposed to a near-fatal brush with witchcraft—in a case so sensational that the effects reverberated for the next hundred years on both sides of the Atlantic.

The story, crawling with eerie omens—and reported instantly and down to the last detail in a blackletter broadside, *Newes from Scotland*—began with James's marriage by proxy to Anne of Denmark in July, 1589. He was twenty-three and she was fifteen. They had never met.

So far, nothing unusual. Quite the normal procedure for royal marriages.

However, when the Princess set out for England, she got only as far as Oslo, Norway, before buffeting winds and storms all but destroyed the ship and stranded her for months. Hearing of her plight, James himself set sail in an English ship, succeeded in meeting his bride—but then was forced by continuing storms to remain in Scandinavia until the spring of 1590. When at last the newlyweds embarked for England, the ship, rocked by still more deadly winds and waves, barely reached its destination.

Scandal erupted. The King's chief enemy, the Earl of Bothwell, his first cousin and also leader of the Catholics, was charged with using witchcraft to destroy the Protestant James at sea in order to seize the throne for himself.

The first to implicate the Earl of Bothwell was a lowly servant girl, Geillis Duncan. She belonged to David Seaton, Deputy Town Bailiff, whose action in torturing her into confession before bringing her story to public attention was obviously aimed at winning the King's favor. A highly believable witness who had already demonstrated an uncanny ability to cure illness, she was also discovered to have a witch's mark on her body. The thirty others she named as her accomplices included a local schoolteacher and three socially prominent women, Catholics all.

What had begun as political rivalry between James and Bothwell, now was couched in supernatural terms describing a huge sabbath, which occurred at the church in North Berwick. Present were two hundred witch-agents of Bothwell, himself transformed into the Devil. Bothwell and the teacher named by Geillis Duncan—Dr. John Fian, mysteriously known also as Dr. John Cunningham—were the only men at the gathering. Dr. Fian confessed under torture to serving the Devil as secretary and reading off the names of those in attendance as recorded in the Devil's book.

Three women were named by Geillis as the leaders of the witches. They were Mrs. Agnes Sampson, a midwife known as the "wise woman of Keith," whom the records described as dignified and matronly and "grave and settled in all her answers"; and her chief assistants Euphame Mackalzeane, daughter of a local nobleman, Lord Cliftonhall, and Barbara Napier. All three testified that Bothwell had presided over the sabbath at which they produced a wax image christened by Agnes Sampson with these words:

> This is King James the Sixth, ordered to be consumed
> at the instance of a nobleman, Francis, Earl of Bothwell.

And Barbara Napier added the information that by casting this spell the witches wished to insure "that another might have ruled in his Majesty's place, and the government might have gone to the Devil."

Agnes Sampson further confessed that the Devil "did greatly inveigh against the King of Scotland, and he received [the witches'] oaths for their good and true service towards him . . . at which time the witches demanded of the Devil, 'Why did he bear such hatred to the King?' Who answered:

'By reason the King is the greatest enemy he hath in the world.' "

At this point, the booklet *Newes from Scotland* notes that "these confessions made the King in wonderful admiration," so that he took a special interest in the case and had all the accused brought before him at his palace in Holyrood. Tortured almost into loss of consciousness, they elaborated on a tale that included going in sieves over the sea, where they raised storms by casting dead cats into water, and concocting poisons to be fed to the King. Agnes Sampson described the Devil as a man with a black beard like the beard of a goat, "who caused all the company to kiss his arse which . . . was cold like ice." She continued:

> His body was hard like iron, as they thought that handled him; his face was terrible, his nose like the beak of an eagle, great burning eye; his hands and legs were hairy, with claws upon his hands and feet like the griffon, and he spoke with a low voice . . . The Devil, clad in a black gown, with a black hat upon his head preached unto a number of them, having lighted candles around him . . . [Several marvelled] that all their deviltry could do no harm to the King, as it did to several others. The Devil answered, "Il est un homme de Dieu." [He is a man of God.] And certainly he is a man of God and does no wrong wittingly, but is inclined to all godliness, justice, and virtue; therefore God has preserved him in the midst of many dangers . . .

Putting French words into the mouth of the Devil—and also Mother Waterhouse's description of childbed in mangled Scots-French (see Chapter Six)—are excellent indications that Continental witchcraft came to Scotland by way of the country's closest ally, France. The widowed queen-regent, French Mary of Guise, had ruled Scotland from 1547–1560, while her daughter, the future Queen Mary, underwent a French education from the age of five. At age sixteen, the younger Mary had married the French Dauphin, in line to be king of France. Widowed at age eighteen, she had returned to Scotland in 1560 as that country's queen, bringing along her French court and a complete repertoire of French witch beliefs.

A whole category of elaborate beliefs connected with the witches' sabbath, imported from the Continent, first made their British appearance in this case. And every detail amounts to a perversion of conventional religious ceremonies. Thus the sabbath took place in a church at North Berwick, on All Hallow's Eve, the thirty-first of October. The Devil, dressed in ministerial black, sat on his throne before a pulpit, giving instructions and orders to commit evil. After worshipping Satan in the usual manner—kissing his hindside—everyone danced back to back, led by Dr. Fian as master of ceremonies, with music played by Geillis Duncan on a kind of miniature trumpet. As the company of two hundred danced, they chanted:

> *Cummer, go ye before, cummer go ye:*
> *If ye will not go before, cummer let me.*

Newes from Scotland leaves nothing to the imagination when describing the torturous searching of Agnes Sampson's body for the witch's mark:

And for as much as by due examination of witchcraft and witches in Scotland, it hath lately been found that the Devil doth generally mark them with a private mark, by reason the witches have confessed themselves, that the Devil doth lick them with his tongue in some privy part of their selves before he doth receive them to be his servants, which mark commonly is given them under the hair in some part of their body, whereby it may not easily be found out or seen, although they be searched; and generally so long as the mark is not seen to those which search them, so long the parties that hath the mark will never confess anything. Therefore, by special commandment this Agnes Sampson had all her hair shaven off, in each part of her body, and her head thrown with a rope . . . being a pain most grievous which she continued almost an hour, during which time she would not confess anything, until the Devil's mark was found upon her privities; then she immediately confessed whatsoever was demanded of her, and justifying those persons aforesaid to be notorious witches.

Toward the end of the trial, the King suddenly turned skeptic, according to the published broadside, refused to believe everything Agnes Sampson told him, and called the whole group "extreme liars." Agnes Sampson took the King's epithet as a personal challenge and so—if the report is to be believed—whispered in his ear the exact conversation between himself and his bride on their wedding night in Oslo. Momentarily speechless with wonder, the King recovered himself to swear "by the living God that he believed all the devils in hell could not have discovered the same, . . . acknowledging her words to be most true and therefore gave the more credit to the rest that is before declared."

The accused witches and Dr. Fian were burned at the stake at the end of January, 1591. With the aid of well-placed friends, the Earl of Bothwell escaped with his life to hide in the Highlands.

THE IMPRESSIONABLE and highly nervous James, watching the case of the North Berwick witches unfold first hand, was further jolted by news of an ongoing trial further to the south in England. In Huntingdon County (near Cambridge) witches from the Warboys area were hunted, examined, tried and executed over a long period from November 10, 1589, to April 5, 1593. (In Elizabeth I's old age, with no successor in sight capable of insuring England's continued glory and stability—plus the all-too-usual disasters of plague, poor harvests, and famine—the Queen could no longer hold off the demons.)

At first glance, the case of the witches of Warboys seems to demonstrate English sophistication as opposed to Scottish superstition. Scotland's North Berwick witches, some two hundred in number, were accused of directing their evil activities against their country's king and of using the latest Continental procedures at their Sabbath. In contrast, only three witches were involved in the England's Warboys trial, no Sabbath took place, several highly placed members of the community refused to believe the charges at first, and the target was not the monarch but the wife of a local political leader.

But, especially in witch-hunts, things are never what they seem.

So first, the facts of the case—as far as revealed by the broadside published at London in 1593, *The Most Strange and Admirable Discovery of the Three Witches of Warboys. . . .* Then, a look at the century-long effects on both sides of the Atlantic.

The case took shape when ten-year-old Jane Throckmorton of Warboys suddenly went into convulsions. Recovering, she caught sight of seventy-six-year-old Alice Samuel, a wrinkled old beggar who came calling frequently to receive food and hand-me-down clothes from wealthy Sir Robert Throckmorton. Immediately, young Jane accused Mother Samuel of causing the fits, a complaint taken up by her four sisters, ranging in age from nine to fifteen, who similarly sickened and denounced the old woman for their troubles.

The parents of the children refused to pay any attention to their ravings—until their longtime friend, Lady Cromwell, wife of Sir Henry Cromwell, one of the wealthiest and most respected men in the area, came to visit, along with her daughter-in-law. Viewing the screaming children and recognizing Mother Samuel as a tenant on her property, Lady Cromwell ripped the bonnet from the old woman's head, ordered her hair burned, and denounced her as a witch.*

"Madam, why do you use me thus? I never did you any harm, as yet," Mother Samuel protested.

Without deigning to answer, Lady Cromwell returned home. And the Throckmorton parents continued to dismiss the charges, ignoring even the threat implied in Mother Samuel's words, "as yet."

In the absence of Sir Henry, Lady Cromwell and her daughter-in-law slept in the same bed that night (a common practice in order to save fuel by shutting off unused rooms). The next morning both told of Lady Cromwell's tormenting nightmare about Mother Samuel: the old woman had sent her familiar, a cat, to tear the skin and flesh from Lady Cromwell's body. All at once, Lady Cromwell began writhing with the fever of a painful illness, dying a lingering death fifteen months later in July, 1592.

The mere logic of the Throckmortons was no match for the terrible death of Lady Cromwell and the constantly replayed writhing fits of their own daughters. Now the authorities questioned Mother Samuel, stripped and shaved her body to examine her for witch's marks, and dragged her back and forth between jail and the Throckmorton household where the sick children touched or scratched her to relieve their fits. Her health failing, her mind cracked, Mother Samuel came to believe that she was indeed a witch: "I have forsaken my maker and given my soul to the Devil," she acknowledged to

* Cf. the New Testament, I Corinthians, 11:6—"Since it is a shameful thing for a woman to shave her head or cut her hair, she should cover her head."

the whole Throckmorton family. Then kissing the children—who now indicated that they would forgive her—she departed.

But after a good night's sleep, she retracted her confession.

Along with her husband John and their daughter Agnes, she was thrown into jail, accused of bewitching the children and killing Lady Cromwell. In addition, several local residents now came forth accusing all three Samuels of killing their livestock.

In a trial lasting exactly five hours, all three were condemned to death as witches. An inkling into the strong-minded stubbornness of young Agnes Samuel comes from her refusal to plead pregnancy in order to postpone her execution:

> Nay, that I will not do: it shall never be said that I was both a witch and a whore.

The execution took place on April 5, 1593.

This case had strong repercussions in the decade that followed. First of all, the influential men involved—especially the Cromwells—served in the first Parliament of James when he became King of Great Britain, in 1603. Thus they helped to write and pass a harsh 1604 statute against witchcraft, the operating law for all of England's seventeenth century witch trials, at home and in the colonies.

Equally important, this case, combined with the Scottish trial of the North Berwick witches, led King James to vent his indignation on the skeptical and mocking treatment displayed by Reginald Scot in *The Discoverie of Witchcraft.* In 1597, James published his own carefully researched tract, *Daemonologie,* adding at the end the broadside *Newes from Scotland.*

BASED ON HIS OWN EXPERIENCE, the King related how witches can cause death by burning a person's picture, make

A witch and her various familiars (demons in the form of animals). From a chapbook illustration, 1621.—COURTESY BRITISH LIBRARY

men and women sick by manipulating wax images, and raise storms at sea or in the air.

Quite readily he accepts that the Devil can appear "in likeness of a dog, a cat, an ape or such-like other beast," thus making any old woman who keeps a dog or cat for company suspected of having a familiar.

He also shows familiarity with the mythological "Diana and her wandering court." But perhaps most significant is the dialogue he carries on with himself on the predominance of women as witches:

> What can be the cause that there are twenty women given to that craft where there is one man?

> Answer: The reason is easy, for as that sex is frailer than man is, so it is easier to be entrapped in these gross snares of the Devil as was ever well proved to be true by the Serpent's deceiving of Eve at the beginning, which makes him the homelier [more at home with] that sex.

Toward the end of his book he adds:

> Where the devil finds greatest ignorance and barbarity . . . there assails he grossliest, as I gave you the reason wherefor there was more witches of women kind than men.

From all this it follows without surprise that James is convinced that women should never be permitted to meddle in politics or to rule over men. In a letter to his young son Henry in 1599 about how to treat a wife, he included this advice:

> Treat her as your own flesh, command her as your Lord, cherish her as your helper, rule her as your pupil, and please her in all things reasonable; but teach her not

to be curious in things that belong her not. You are the head, she is your body. It is your office to command and hers to obey . . . Women are the frailest sex.*

In 1603, James left Scotland forever to sit on the throne once occupied by Queen Elizabeth. In 1604, he saw to it that the old witchcraft law was strengthened. The single most important addition was punishment by death for a witch (usually a woman, according to James's own book *Daemonologie*) who made a pact with the Devil.

Increasingly, political scientists theorized and men believed that government was based on a compact or contract between God and men who were strong, virtuous, and intelligent. If women who were weak, prey to temptation (since Eve), and stupid should ever make a similar pact with the Devil, they would have unlimited power, but only to produce evil rather than good, anarchy instead of stability. In other words, men went round and round in circles, using the same arguments to exclude women from political power and to execute them for witchcraft.

But is was not enough merely to execute witches. Their supporters, too, had to be silenced. For example, although Reginald Scot had died in 1599, his skeptical book about witchcraft was considered a continuing threat. Thus all copies were ordered rounded up for burning by the public executioner—though there must have been several that were successfully hidden, judging from the number of later writers who cited Scot.

* James apparently liked this particular reference from the New Testament (. . . "the head of every man is Christ; and the head of the woman is the man." I Corinthians, 11:3) He carried the idea into government, telling Parliament on March 19, 1604, in his first speech after coronation as King of Great Britain: "I am the husband and the whole isle [Scotland, Wales, and England] is my lawful wife. I am the head and it is my body."

Pope Joan and a companion dressed in their ecclesiastical robes,
hang over the jaws of hell. Joan clasps her newborn infant to
her breast. To the left of the gallows two demons stand guard.
Beyond these, sinners are being consumed by flames.

It is reported that this Joan was a female and that she conceived
by one of her servants. The Pope, becoming pregnant, gave birth
to a child, wherefore some do not number her among the
Pontiffs.—SIGEBERT DE GEMBLOURS, C. 1110

The legend of Pope Joan began with a mere mention by a
ninth century contemporary who had died in 886. A second
reference appeared when Marianus Scotus who died in 1086
wrote that in 854 "Joanna, a woman, succeeded Leo [847–854]
and reigned two years, five months, and four days."

The story grew bigger and better in the hands of several later
chroniclers, till by the thirteenth century Martin Polonus was
writing that Joan had studied for three years at Rome, after which
her pupils included "great masters":

> And when there arose a high opinion in the city of her
> virtue and knowledge, she was unanimously elected pope. But

during her papacy, she became in the family way by a familiar. Not knowing the time of birth, as she was on her way from Saint Peter's to the Lateran she had a painful delivery between the Coliseum and Saint Clement's Church in the street. Having died after, it is said that she was buried on the spot, and therefore the Lord Pope always turns aside from that way, and it is supposed by some, out of detestation for what happened there. Nor on that account is she placed in the catalogue of the Holy Pontiffs, not only on account of her sex, but also because of the horribleness of the circumstance.

With the Reformation of the sixteenth century, Protestants latched on to the legend to vilify the Catholics. And in the early seventeenth century, the vicar of Leeds, England, Alexander Cooke, published *Pope Joane* in the form of a quaint debate in which a nameless English "Protestant" demolished all the arguments of a similarly anonymous "Papist." Cooke sums up the case, proving that the historical existence of Pope Joan had badly undermined the Catholic Church:

> How can your priests be assured that they were priested by lawful bishops and how can you lay papists be assured that you are absolved by lawful priests, or that your masses are said by lawful priests, seeing we read (as before I showed) that Pope Joan gave orders, Pope Joan made deacons and priests, and bishops, and abbots. For it may be well enough that the priests of this present age are descended from those who were ordered by her: especially seeing we nowhere read that they were degraded by succeeding popes, who had their ordination from her.

Well-trained in disputation and debate at Oxford where he had received both his bachelor's and master's degrees, Rev. Cooke demonstrated to his own and his readers' satisfaction that a woman named Joan had indeed occupied the papacy, once the most high and most masculine position of power. The moral was clear, an unarguable precedent for excluding women from power.

This book was part of the Mather Library in Boston, Massachusetts.

CHAPTER EIGHT

"More Women, More Witches"

The idea of the witch's pact with the Devil made the rounds at the very same time as the idea of the divine right of kings—traveling the identical route from the Continent to Scotland to England.

Whereas Queen Elizabeth had manipulated Parliament by a shrewd combination of tact, compromise, and flattery, James, whose Scottish upbringing was forever getting in his way, snarled at Parliament in 1610:

> Kings are justly called gods for that they exercise a manner of resemblance of divine power upon earth . . . They make and unmake their subjects; they have power of raising and casting down; of life and of death; judges over all their subjects and in all causes, and yet accountable to none but God only . . . As to dispute what God may do is blasphemy, so it is sedition in subjects to dispute what a king might do in height of his power.

Still, even as God's agent, the King faced grave challenges—from the agents of the Devil, the witches. They were forever promising the Devil their services in return for the power to make or destroy anything they pleased. Anybody looking around England could all too easily find evidence of the ruination being wreaked on England by these witches working for the Devil. For example, no sooner had the country recovered from its worst—and longest—period of famine in a century of bad harvests, the starving time of 1593–1597, than the dreaded plague of the Middle Ages returned, killing one person out of five in London alone. Also, widespread death and illness prevented Parliament from meeting for almost a year after the King's arrival.

FRANTICALLY SEARCHING for a cure-all, James had Parliament pass a new witchcraft statute as its very first order of business—just eight days after it finally came into session in 1604. James prescribed hanging for a whole group of activities that Elizabeth had dismissed as *maleficia* (evil-doing), and he also added some new capital offenses. *Maleficia* included causing harm—though not death—to persons or animals, or destroying property, or making love potions to snag an unwilling male into marriage. For the first conviction, under Elizabeth, the culprit received one year of imprisonment, plus four sessions of six hours each in the pillory at the public marketplace. Only for the second conviction or for outright murder would the penalty be death. Crimes not mentioned in the Elizabethan statute but punishable by hanging in James's reign were making a pact with the Devil and/or keeping familiars.

In the first fifteen years of James's reign the number hanged annually for witchcraft was several times the number executed in each of the last years of Elizabeth's rule. Even more important, over forty percent of those executed under the statute passed in 1604 would have avoided death under the Elizabethan law of 1563.

James's witchcraft statute was further reinforced by publication of William Perkins's *Discourse on the Damned Art of Witchcraft*. Impelled by the case of the Witches of Warboys (Lady Cromwell *vs.* Mother Samuel), which he had observed firsthand and recorded in detail, Rev. Perkins finished his book while Elizabeth was still alive and reigning. But perhaps because he included so many ideas from James's *Daenonologie*—especially the pact with the Devil—publication was held up until 1608, five years after James's accession to the English throne, six years after Perkins's own demise. The witch's pact with the Devil, Perkins insisted, "is a most evident and certain truth that may not be called into question." This makes a witch more powerful than even a monarch, Perkins claimed.

James had asserted that witches were mostly women; Perkins proved the contention, and explained why Moses used the feminine gender in making the law against witches (Exodus 22:18: "Thou shalt not suffer a witch to live."):

First, to give us to understand that the woman being the weaker sex is sooner entangled by the Devil's illusions with this damnable act than the man. And in all ages it is found true by experience that the Devil has more easily and oftener prevailed with women than with men. Hence it was that the Hebrews of ancient times used it for a proverb, *The More women, the more witches.* [Italics inserted by Perkins.]

As did King James and many other contemporaries, Perkins advocated the never-fail test of "swimming a witch." She would be tossed into the water, right thumb bound to left toe, left thumb to right toe (a widely used practice on the Continent, beginning in the mid-sixteenth century). If she sank—and presumably drowned—that meant the pure water accepted her, and so she was not a witch. If she floated, she was definitely a candidate for the hangman's noose. Either way she had no future.

NOW CAME the most famous witch prosecution of James's reign, the trial of the witches of Lancaster in 1612—brimful of pacts with the Devil and familiars in the guises of dogs named Tibb and Ball. Fifteen witches were accused in a trial that (1) added to the King's authoritativeness; (2) made a long-lasting impression on the very same Puritan inhabitants of the area who would soon be leaving to found Massachusetts Bay Colony; and (3) formed the subject matter of an instant bestseller published in 1613—*The Wonderful Discoverie of Witches in the County of Lancaster,* the most complete eyewitness account of any English witchcraft prosecution. Author Thomas Potts, clerk of the court, strewed the factual narration with his own running commentary and spicy descriptions, thus dehumanizing the accused women, turning them into the familiar stereotype: female, frighteningly ugly, destructive, and a threat to society. The entire case, author Potts declared, was based on "what the King's Majesty has written and published in his *Daemonologie*."

Close reading of the account reveals a feud to the death between two families living in the wilds of Pendle Forest, located in the lonely hills of eastern Lancashire. Two eighty-year-old women were pitted against each other as ringleaders. One was Elizabeth Sowthernes, also known as Mother Demdike. Potts describes her as an old widow, reduced to begging for a living. Labeling her a "damnable and malicious witch" and also a "sink of villainy and mischief," he notes that she had been "a witch for fifty years":

Thus lived she securely for many years, brought up her own children, instructed her grandchildren, and took great care and pains to bring them to be witches. She was a general agent for the Devil in all these parts; no man escaped her, or her Furies, that ever gave them any occasion to offense, or denied them anything they stood need of. And certain it is, no man near them was secure or free from danger.

The other principal in the case he names as "Anne Whittle," alias "Chattox":

> A very old, withered, spent, and decrepit creature, her sight almost gone; a dangerous witch of very long continuance, always opposed to Old Demdike: for whom the one favored the other hated deadly . . .
>
> In her witchcraft, always more ready to do mischief to men's goods, than themselves. Her lips ever chattering and walking, but no man knew what. She lived in the Forest of Pendle, amongst this wicked company of dangerous witches . . .
>
> I place her in order next to that wicked fire-brand of mischief, old Demdike, because from these two sprung all the rest in order, and were the children and friends of these two notorious witches.

The case began when Mother Demdike's granddaughter, Alison Device, accused Anne Redfearn, married daughter of Old Chattox, of stealing some of her belongings. Amid accusations and counter-accusations both old women were arrested. Shortly after, Alison Device and Anne Redfearn were likewise taken prisoner. The four were locked up together in Lancaster Castle where Mother Demdike soon died.

Meanwhile, at a safe distance from the Castle, both families decided to work together to free the prisoners. Agreeing to meet at a mysterious place called Malkin Tower in Pendle Forest, eighteen women and two men—a most interesting sex ratio—gathered for a kind of sabbath where they feasted on beef, bacon, and roast mutton. No doubt remembering the recent infamous Gunpowder Plot—an unsuccessful attempt in

November, 1605, by Catholic fanatic Guy Fawkes to blow up King and Parliament—these twenty now planned to rescue their own relatives by blowing up the local castle and killing the lord of the manor, Robert Nutter. This third family, the Nutters, got into the act when their son Christopher attempted to seduce the already-married Anne Redfearn. Her rejection made him threaten to evict her whole family from their tiny piece of land as soon as he inherited his father's feudal holdings. When Anne's mother threatened young Nutter with death by witchcraft, he did in fact die within three months. The father, Robert Nutter, then actively entered the case.

Justice of the Peace, Roger Nowell, ordered twelve of the company arrested and brought to trial, along with the three prisoners from the Castle. Chief witness was a nine-year-old girl, Jennet Device, daughter of Elizabeth—whose hanging she insured by her testimony—and granddaughter of the safely dead Mother Demdike. Jennet, considered too young to join the sabbath, apparently had kept all the details in her remarkably retentive and inventive memory.

The exact method of using an image to procure death by witchcraft was carefully described:

Make a picture of clay, like unto the shape of the person whom they mean to kill, and dry it thoroughly; and when they would have them to be ill in any one place more than another, then take a thorn or pin, and prick it in that part of the picture you would so have to be ill; and when you would have any part of the body to consume away, then take that part of the picture, and burn it. And when they would have the whole body to consume away, then take the remnant of the said picture, and burn it, and so thereupon by that means, the body shall die.

Ten were put to death as witches following this trial, the three Castle prisoners plus five women and two men who had met at Malkin Tower.

Proving that history writes the best drama of all, one of those put to death was Alice Nutter. She was the daughter-in-law of Robert Nutter, lord of the manor and prime mover behind the prosecution—and sister-in-law of Christopher Nutter, the young heir who was supposedly bewitched to death. The charge against Alice Nutter was that she had actively helped in the defense of the accused witches.

At this point, it is disappointing to have to report that the official record of her trial recounts nothing more than her refusal to confess or to give testimony against others:

Her own children were never able to move her to confess any particular offense or declare anything . . . which was a very fearful thing to all that were present who knew she was guilty.

In any event, the hanging of this wealthy woman alongside nine who were extremely poor again reveals witch inquisitors unmoved by social status. Also, her death as a convicted witch (most probably because she had dared to defend others accused of witchcraft) harks back to the admonition of Jean Bodin—recently translated from French into English—that witches were to be executed if only as an example to others.

BY 1614, KING JAMES was ruling England with an iron hand, exuding confidence in all his actions and speeches. Sometime after 1615, he began exhibiting definite doubts about witches and their powers for evil. Several cases are on record that the King exposed witches as suffering from nothing more than the "mother," an old fifteenth-century term for hysteria (which in turn is a word derived from the Greek "hystera," meaning "womb"). And in other cases he found solid evidence of imposture.

However, James, steeped in Scottish folklore and seventeenth century English superstition, never gave up his beliefs so completely as to withdraw *Daemonologie* from circulation or to retract anything he had written in the book. Nor did he make any move to repeal his 1604 statute on witchcraft.

Many poor women imprifoned, and hanged for Witches.
Hangman. B. *Belman.* C. *Two Sergeants.* D. *Witch-*
der taking his money for his work.

Here women are on the gallows or awaiting their turn. Men
surround them, ready to act in their various capacities, named in
the caption below the picture. Conspicuous is the witch-finder at
the right, in the act of accepting money for his work. On the
left behind bars are three terrified observers, one a small child, as
though to point out that witches inevitably spawn
daughter-witches.

PRINT PUBLISHED 1655—COURTESY BRITISH LIBRARY

CHAPTER NINE

"Witchfinder General"

Sometimes tales of witchcraft are both folk and tall. Especially those that array males who are supermen against a lone woman who breathes supernatural defiance.

Take this story, for example, about a witch captured by soldiers in the middle of England's Civil War. In 1643, a woman was seen walking on a plank over water at Newbury, some sixty miles west of London. When the Puritan group commanders ordered two soldiers to shoot her immediately for practicing witchcraft, she defiantly caught the bullets in her hand and began to chew them. The soldiers tried again, putting the rifle close to her breast, only to have the bullet ricochet, narrowly missing their own faces. Next, they took after her with a sword, but she, laughing at them, escaped again. Her downfall was a soldier who remembered that even the mightiest witch could be destroyed by cutting the veins across the forehead to draw blood. Thus threatened, the woman knew she could no longer count on the Devil to save her, and began loudly to groan, moan, and roar, crying that she must now certainly die. The soldiers shot her to death through the ear and left her body to the worms. George Hammond who first wrote down this story in 1643 concluded piously:

> Her soul we ought not to judge of, though the evils of her wicked life and death can escape no censure.

The story was, of course, a product of the seventeenth century—and of wartime. (It was widely circulated, orally and in print. By 1929 it was included in the classic study *Witch Hunting and Witch Trials,* a collection of records and folktales by England's pioneer scholar, C. L'Estrange Ewen.)

Since the original author resorted to the supernatural, and for good measure added pious insult, the modern mind should consider two solid inferences: (1) Soldiers are always woman-starved. (2) In wartime, while men are off fighting, females often follow soldiers to camp and battlefield, begging food and shelter for themselves and their children. Now fill in this woman's side of the story, using all the empty spaces between the lines—and then pass judgment.

ANOTHER BYPRODUCT of the Civil War was Matthew Hopkins who proclaimed himself "Witchfinder General" of eastern England in March, 1645. He sent some two hundred witches to the gallows in Essex and other Puritan counties in the fourteen months before his own (natural) death in May, 1646.

Two curious consequences followed. First, Hopkins turned witchfinding into a profitable vocation. At a time when the average pay was sixpence per day, he gave his assistants—one male and four females—twice the going rate, or one shilling for a day's work. And he himself is recorded as receiving six pounds (one pound equaled twenty shillings) for his expedition to Aldeburgh and twenty-three pounds for a trip to Stowmarket.

The second and more lasting result was that Hopkins made English-speaking witch-hunts synonymous with Puritanism. This was especially true in America where witch-hunting was just getting under way in the 1640s.

IN THE YEAR 1664, Sir Matthew Hale, Chief Justice of England, cleared away the final hurdle necessary for the later

Salem witchcraft trials. He set the strongest possible precedent for admitting testimony based on spectral evidence. Accepted without even a raised eyebrow were stories of seeing the body of the accused sitting, standing, or sleeping in bed, while at the same time viewing her specter flying off to a sabbath, or swinging from a beam in the ceiling, or walking in the fields and streets to destroy property or commit murder. Added would be descriptions of the Devil appearing in the shape of various familiars: spiders, flies, ants, dogs, cats, or rats.

Everything about Justice Hale made him seem a model of moderation and respectability. A veteran of the Puritan Parliament in the 1650s when Oliver Cromwell had ruled as Lord Protector of the Commonwealth of England, Hale was knighted by Charles II after the Restoration of monarchy in 1660. Before assuming the position of Chief Justice he had been one of England's most prominent and effective lawyers, participating in many of the great political cases of the era.

But there he was in 1664 at Bury St. Edmunds (home territory in the early seventeenth century for Massachusetts's first governor, Puritan John Winthrop), presiding at the trial for witchcraft of Amy Duny and Rose Cullender.

Every stock stereotype is present in this trial: old women accused as witches; children as accusers acting on behalf of angry men; a learned, highly respected male judge who uses a jury of women to examine the accused for witch marks; and a court reporter who has no hesitation in adding his own opinions to the words spoken at the trial. There are two more indispensable similarities: (1) The young girls who are the chief witnesses in court have public fits of hysteria, and they rely heavily on special evidence. (2) One of the accused old women, Amy Duny, was related to a woman previously put to death at Bury St. Edmunds, in 1645, during the witch-hunt conducted by Matthew Hopkins.

The initial accusation against old Rose Cullender was made by a yeoman farmer, John Soam, who was using three carts for his harvest. When one cart broke loose, accidentally shattering the window of Rose Cullender's house, she rushed out in a rage, screaming and threatening him with revenge. Shortly afterwards the first two carts proceeded on their way, loading and unloading as usual, but the offending vehicle refused to work properly, getting stuck in awkward places, and requiring unloading far away from the usual spot. When some friends tried to help in the unloading, their noses began bleeding so hard that they had to abandon the cart till the next morning.

A second man, Robert Sherringham, accused Rose Cullender of responsibility for filling his clothing with such big lice—two years before—that he had to burn his suits to stop the creatures from swarming around his skin. These of course were years when soap was scarce. Worse, plague epidemics frightened everyone with their regular recurrence.

The accusation against Amy Duny was quite different, but equally sensational. Babysitting for the wife of a local tradesman, she had nursed the child against the mother's orders. When the baby fell into convulsions that night, the attending Dr. Jacob blamed Amy Duny and prescribed wrapping the baby in a blanket and burning anything that dropped out. Finding a toad—long the incarnation of evil—the doctor threw it into the fire where it burned with "a flashing in the fire like gunpowder," singeing Amy's face, legs, and thighs, and thus sealing her guilt.

Another time, Amy cursed her employer for discharging her. The two children who were to be her chief witnesses at the trial heard the curse and began to suffer severe afflictions, throwing up pins and nails, duly offered as evidence. (Pins, which played a similar role at the Salem trials, are today displayed in a special showcase at the Salem Superior Court.)

At the trial the children went into fits every time they saw the two women or their specters, which were invisible to everyone else present. When a cynic sought to disprove the children's testimony by blindfolding them and substituting strangers, the young girls immediately identified the newcomers as Amy Duny and Rose Cullender. At this point the court reporter inserted himself into the record. Echoing the father of the young girls, he gave his considered opinion that the young girls might be led by the two witches to think that they had touched them—even when they had not done so.

MEANWHILE ON THE LITERARY SCENE, English playwright Thomas Heywood wrote a 651 page book titled *The General History of Women* which first went into circulation in 1657. Though he is cynical on the subject of witchcraft (in fact he had written a play parodying the trial of the Lancashire Witches), he manages to do a great disservice to women as he recounts without comment all current myths, superstitions, and the works of such witch-tract writers as Bodin and Fathers Sprenger and Kramer, authors of the *Malleus*. He describes fully the exploits of the mythological Amazons, Circe, and Medea; the Biblical villainy of Jezebel and Delilah; and the earthly bellicosity of Joan of Arc.

Concluding his chapter Of Amazons and Warlike Women, he remarks:

> I know not better how to express the boldness of women than by showing you the fear of men.

ONLY ONE WOMAN in the seventeenth century, Jane Sharp, comes even close to answering the centuries of slander that made females prime candidates for execution as witches. Plunging right in without wasting a word of type, Mrs. Sharp uses the title page of her book to describe the subject matter as well as her own qualifications for writing: "The Midwives Book of the Whole Art of Midwifery Discovered, Directing Childbearing Women How to Behave Themselves in Their

Conception, Breeding, Bearing, and Nursing of Children. By Mrs. Jane Sharp, Practitioner in the Art of Midwifery above Thirty Years. London, Printed for Simon Miller, at the Star of the West End of St. Pauls, 1671."

In 418 pages, Mrs. Sharp demonstrates profound knowledge of male and female anatomy, the Bible, and mythology. In a kind of note to the reader she writes: "Sisters, I have often sat down, sad in the consideration of the many miseries women endure in the hands of unskillful midwives, many professing the art (without any skill in anatomy, which is the principal part effectually necessary for a midwife) merely for lucres sake . . ."

She contends that only women should be midwives:

Some perhaps may think that then it is not proper for women to be of this profession, because they cannot attain so rarely to the knowledge of things as men may, who are bred up in Universities, schools of learning, or serve their apprenticeships for that end and purpose, where anatomy lectures being frequently read, the situation of the parts both of men and women and other things of great consequence are often made plain to them . . . It is commendable for men to employ their spare time in some things of deeper speculation than is required of the female sex; but the art of midwifery chiefly concerns us, which even the best learned men will grant, yielding something of their own to us, when they are forced to borrow from us the very name they practice by, and to call themselves *Men-midwives* . . . it is commonly maintained that the masculine gender is more worthy than the feminine, though perhaps when men have need of us they will yield the priority to us.

Subtly responding to the repeated masculine claims that women are the superstitious sex and that a couple's childlessness is the fault of the wife, she dismisses an old tale about male barrenness. In bawdy English the Restoration Court must have taken to its heart, she declares:

> There is barrenness by enchantment, when a man cannot lie with his wife by reason of some charm that hath disabled him: the French in such case advise a man to thread the needle, as much as to say, to piss through his wife's wedding ring and not spill a drop and then he shall be perfectly cured. Let him try it that pleaseth.

Best of all she disputes centuries of taboos and fears of menstruation:

> Some say this blood is venomous, and will poison plants it falls upon, discolour a fair looking glass by the breath of her that hath her courses, and comes but near to breathe upon the glass; that ivory will be obscured by it. It hath strong qualities indeed when it is mixed with ill humours. But were the blood venomous in itself it could not remain a full month in the woman's body and not hurt her; nor yet the infant, after conception, for then it flows not forth, but serves for the child's nutriment.

Jane Sharp's book was a forecast of the Age of Reason, which would envelop England, Europe, and the New World by the eighteenth century.

The following decade, in 1682, playwright Thomas Shadwell (1642–1692) was using the theater to laugh witchcraft right out of existence in England—with an assist from the scientific revolution and increasing political enlightenment. Coming from the heart of witch country (he was born in Norfolk and educated at Bury St. Edmund's School and Caius College, Cambridge), Shadwell included this scene in his comedy *The Lancashire Witches and Tegue O'Divelly the*

Irish Priest. The speakers were "Sir Jeffrey Shacklehead, a simple Justice, pretending to great skill in Witches, and a great persecutor of them" and "Sir Edward Hartford, a worthy, hospitable, true English Gentleman of good understanding and honest principles."

SIR EDWARD: Dreams, mere dreams of witches, old women's fables; the devil's not such a fool as you would make him . . .

SIR JEFFREY: No witches! Why I have hanged above fourscore. Read Bodin, Remy, Delrio, Nider, Kramer, Sprenger, Godelman, and More, and Malleus Maleficarum, a great author that writes sweetly about witches, very sweetly.

SIR EDWARD: Malleus Maleficarum a writer! He has read nothing but the titles, I see.

SIR JEFFREY: Oh, a great man! Malleus was a great man. Read, Cousin, read the antidote against atheism: Well, I'll make work among your witches.

Unfortunately, instead of reading this satire, Cotton Mather —New England's intellectual witch hunter—was busy with a powerful witchcraft tract that came out about the same time, Joseph Glanvill's *Saducimus Triumphatus or Full and Plain Evidence Concerning Witches and Apparitions.* This was an attempt, more successful in the New World than the Old, to put superstition and witch belief on an unshakeable scientific foundation and which tried to respond to the two recently published logical refutations of witchcraft: John Wagstaffe who in 1669 wrote *The Question of Witchcraft Debated;* and *The Displaying of Supposed Witchcraft* by a medical doctor, John Webster (1677).

JEZEBEL

The nastiest epithet Governor John Winthrop of Massachusetts

could hurl at the troublesome Anne Hutchinson was "Jezebel."
The Bible tells the story of this willful queen who led Israel into
idol worship:

And Ahab the son of Omri did evil in the sight of the Lord above all that were before him.

And it came to pass, as if it had been a light thing for him to walk in the sins of Jeroboam the son of Nebat, that he took to wife Jezebel the daughter of Ethbaal king of the Zidonians, and went and served Baal [the chief god of the Canaanites, who was identified with idol-worship by Christians], and worshipped him . . . And Ahab made a grove; and Ahab did more to provoke the Lord God of Israel to anger than all the kings of Israel that were before him.—I KINGS, 16:30–31, 33

"The Story of Jehu, Jezebel, and the Sons of Ahab" is the subject of a tapestry woven in Tournai, France, in the third quarter of the fifteenth century. In those days a tapestry served two functions: insulation for cold castle walls; and a conversation piece, challenging viewers to recall as much as they could of ancient Biblical stories.

Jezebel was a Phoenician princess who married King Ahab of Israel in the ninth century B.C. To promote the worship of her own gods, Baal and Asherah, she ordered the building of shrines everywhere, even in the royal palace. This was her doom, depicted in the tapestry by scenes swirling around her—simultaneously. In the upper left-hand corner, Jehu, the army commander, enters the city of Jezreel. In the lower left is Ahab's ill-fated son, Jehoram—who was to bear the consequences for his father's sin of following Jezebel's wishes—is wounded while riding in his chariot. In the upper right, a messenger delivers a letter directing all the remaining sons of Ahab to be put to death. Then in the bottom right, a servant displays the heads of those slain sons in chests.

Jezebel stands in the center of the maelstrom, peering from a large window. Surrounding her are all the men who decide her fate. She is flanked on either side by the two eunuchs who are about to hurl her out the window to her death below. In an ironic twist, these eunuchs were the priests of Baal and Asherah, indicating that even Jezebel's own gods could not save her.

The action to the left of Jezebel occurred before her death, to the right, afterwards. She is the pivotal point of the entire tapestry—a suitable position because, as the Bible intimates, if not for her, the worship of Baal and Asherah would never have seeped so freely into Israel where it contaminated the kingship itself, so that God's only recourse was to destroy the house of Ahab.—COURTESY ISABELLA STEWART GARDNER MUSEUM, BOSTON

In the late seventeenth century, John Wagstaffe whose writing was well known in both old and New England defined witchcraft in terms of the deeds of Jezebel:

Thus you shall often meet in the Bible with fornication and witchcraft joined together. By fornication and whoredom is meant idolatry and by witchcraft the art of engaging men in it. The whoredom of Jezebel was her idolatry, and her witchcraft was the maintaining of Baal's priests.

CHAPTER TEN

"This American Jezebel"

Cotton Mather, preacher extraordinary of Boston, had a fatal flaw—the same one dragging America's early hero, Gov. John Winthrop, from his lofty pedestal. Both were constantly being scared out of their wits by women and witchcraft and proclaiming their fright publicly.

Admittedly, these were fears shared by most seventeenth century men. Still, the inability of these otherwise great leaders to rise above popular passions is more than a little disconcerting. Most of the time, John Winthrop, the Bay Colony's first governor, displayed high-minded ingenuity and perseverance as he made Massachusetts a shining precedent for future American democracy. And Cotton Mather was a true Renaissance man, more than a century after that remarkable era had drawn to a close. His titles, all earned through high scholarship and tireless work, included "minister," "doctor," "author," and "scientist."

"Suspicion of witchcraft," an exhausted Governor Winthrop moaned in the privacy of his own diary when a woman, Anne Hutchinson, challenged the political establishment of the colony. At any point in the seventeenth century, Anne Hutchinson's ideas—plus her audacity, as a mere woman, in attempting to assume political leadership and power—would have raised a furor of outrage and cries for her immediate repression. But the years, 1634–1637, saw a whole series of near-fatal crises, and as a result Mistress Hutchinson's activities raised the fever of anxiety to a state of delirium. (In 1634 there had been an effort by Charles I to recall the charter that gave Massachusetts Bay complete independence of the mother country. However, the King was three thousand miles away in England and too busy fending off civil war at home to carry out his threat. In 1635, Roger Williams, a thirty-year-old Salem minister, began questioning white claims to Indian land and Church–State relations. Permanent banishment took care of him. And in 1637, two months of widespread slaughter, lasting from May 26 to July 28 and known as the Pequot War, ended with the bitter victory of the better organized colonists over the scattered and disunited Indian tribes of New England.)

HISTORY'S FAVORITE GAME always starts with the words "What if . . ." An excellent way to view contradictions and life-and-death ironies.

Thus, what if Anne Hutchinson had been a man instead of a woman?

Given the series of crises they had just undergone, would the colonial fathers have reacted in the same way? Maybe. Maybe not. Though it is most interesting that in the recently concluded case of Roger Williams there were no references to his maleness as there were in the proceedings against Anne Hutchinson to her femaleness.

There is no question, however, that Anne Hutchinson acted as she did because of her own femaleness.

Like many other early colonists who were female, she had great hopes for Massachusetts Bay when the colony set itself up as a New World utopia in 1630. Massachusetts had no intrenched traditions holding women down—and wilderness living demanded their special skills.

In fact, the Bay Colony positively pampered its women during the first decade or so to insure their migration and settlement. From the beginning, no man was allowed to beat his wife, unless she attacked him first. This was absolutely revolutionary, since Europe for centuries had stressed wife-beating as indispensable to successful marriage. Other Bay Colony laws and judicial decisions forbade a man to desert his wife, or to abandon her in a remote area, "else the town will pull his house down." And courts levied fines on husbands who called their wives servants.

But domestic partnership was one thing. Female participation in public affairs was another, and completely unthinkable. Among other reasons, the colonial fathers argued, women's minds were geared solely to successful homemaking. For example, John Winthrop found that Anne Hopkins, whom he had just met for the first time, had lost her sanity "by occasion of her giving herself wholly to reading and writing and had written many books":

> If she had attended her household affairs and such things as belong to women, and not gone out of her way and calling to meddle in such things as are proper for men whose minds are stronger, etc., she had kept her wits, and might have improved them usefully and honorably in the place God had set her. . . .

John Winthrop and his like-minded cohorts were driven to frenzy when Anne Hutchinson attempted to practice the nonconformity for which they had founded the colony, and which they so often bragged about.

"You have maintained a meeting and an assembly in your house that hath been condemned by the general assembly [legislature] as a thing not tolerable nor comely in the sight of God nor fitting for your sex," Governor Winthrop intoned in his opening courtroom statement when Anne Hutchinson was brought to trial for heresy in November, 1637. At a time when there was absolutely no distinction between church and state—both had the same members, the same pact with God, the same church-meeting house—the Governor accused her of having "troubled the peace of the commonwealth and the churches here."

Right under the nose of Governor Winthrop, Anne Hutchinson, whose house was directly across the street from his, had been holding meetings once or twice a week, radically reinterpreting Puritanism. Well known in the community as a skilled midwife and practitioner of medicine since her arrival in the fall of 1634, she attracted as many as one hundred women, and some men too, as she discussed and dissected the minister's most recent sermon. New England's ebullient eyewitness historian, Edward Johnson of Woburn, quoted one of her admirers, a male:

> Come along with me. . . . I'll bring you to a woman
> that preaches better gospel than any of your black coats
> that have been at the ninneversity.

But Governor Winthrop and the other magistrates were not so sure. They brought Anne Hutchinson to trial where one after another rose to remind the court of events just about a hundred years before, 1520–1534, in Münster, Germany. There, an overwhelming number of women had taken part in a long, bloody Anabaptist rebellion, similarly trying to change the direction of church and state.

Deputy Governor Thomas Dudley complained:

> About three years ago we were all in peace. Mistress
> Hutchinson, from that time she came, hath made a dis-
> turbance and . . . within a half year after, she had
> vented divers of her strange opinions, and had made
> parties [factions] in the country.

The trial of Anne Hutchinson lasted two days, with Governor Winthrop acting as both prosecutor and chief judge. His charges ranged from the sublime—conduct "greatly prejudicial to the state"—to the sneering—holding meetings for women with the results "that families should be neglected . . . and so much time spent [lost]." Under interrogation, Anne Hutchinson did so well that an admiring recent biographer of John Winthrop, Yale historian Edmund S. Morgan, commented that she was the Governor's "intellectual superior in everything except political judgment, in everything except the sense of what was possible in this world." In the end, her sentence was banishment from the colony "as being a woman not fit for our society."

Next came excommunication by the church, a severe punishment signifying permanent loss of God's protection and relegation of the soul to hell upon death. At this final proceeding, just in case anybody missed the point that Anne Hutchinson was stepping out of her bounds as a woman, the Reverend Hugh Peter of Salem scoffed:

> You have rather been a husband than a wife; and a preacher than a hearer; and a magistrate than a subject; and so you have thought to carry all things in church and commonwealth as you would.

Following her trial and excommunication, Anne Hutchinson, now forty-eight, suffered a painful miscarriage. A "monstrous birth," John Winthrop snorted to his diary, certain that this proved her witchcraft. ("Monstrous" in the seventeenth century meant "that which has a divine omen, indicating misfortune.") Matching each of her witchlike heresies, she gave birth to some twenty-seven horrible lumps, "everyone of them greatly confused and . . . altogether without form," ranging in size from "a small Indian bean" to "two male fists."

Anne Hutchinson went to live in Rhode Island. But after a

few years, under somewhat mysterious circumstances, she departed for Long Island. In 1643, she was murdered by Indians, who were angered at all whites for driving them from their land.

Thomas Welde, minister of Roxbury reacted to the news of her murder:

> God's hand is the more apparently seen herein to pick out this woeful woman to make her and those belonging to her an unheard-of heavy example above others.

Similarly spewing more anti-feminism than human sympathy, Governor Winthrop in a widely circulated pamphlet denounced Anne Hutchinson as "this American Jezebel." Still rankling over her attempted takeover of political leadership, he wrote that she "kept her strength and reputation, even among the people of God, till the hand of civil justice laid hold on her, and then she began evidently to decline." In his summation he included such accusations as "her undervaluing of the ordinance of magistracy and ministracy," and labeled her preaching "vomit," which was spurred by the "subtlety of Satan."

INDICATIONS OF STRONG REPERCUSSIONS from Anne Hutchinson's leadership keep popping up in colonial writings. Startling statements came out of Governor Winthrop's own home in Boston, in a letter from his devoted wife Margaret. (Winthrop at the time was in Cambridge, a tedious half-day's journey away, but a friendlier place to hold Anne Hutchinson's trial, he decided, than Boston, which was so full of her supporters.) Datelining her letter "Sad Boston," Margaret Winthrop revealed her innermost feelings:

> Sad thoughts possess my spirits and I cannot repulse them: which makes me unfit for anything, wondering

what the Lord means by all these troubles among us. Sure I am that all shall work to the best to them that love God, or rather are loved by him. I know He will bring light out of obscurity and make his righteousness shine forth as clear as the noonday. *Yet I find in myself an adverse spirit, and a trembling heart, not so willing to submit to the will of God as I desire.* [Emphasis added.]

New England's usually enthusiastic historian, Edward Johnson, sounded a bitterly sarcastic note reporting the further activities of Anne Hutchinson's followers in Rhode Island:

Some of the female sex . . . (deeming the Apostle Paul to be too strict in not permitting a woman to preach in the public congregation)* taught notwithstanding, they having their call to this office from an ardent desire of being famous . . .

BY THE LATE 1640s, Massachusetts turned to the death penalty for troublesome women. Anne Hutchinson had narrowly missed prosecution and execution as a witch—probably because the colony had hardly had enough time to become firmly established and stabilized. But in 1648, eleven years after banishing Anne Hutchinson, the Bay Colony tried its first witch, Margaret Jones of Charlestown.

Unfortunately, none of the writers who knew Margaret Jones or who witnessed her trial and execution for witchcraft thought to describe her as a person, or to explain why she was prosecuted. But John Winthrop filled his Journal with the

---

* "Let your women keep silence in the churches: for it is not permitted unto them to speak; but they are commanded to be under obedience, as also sayeth the law.

"And if they will learn anything, let them ask their husbands at home: for it is a shame for women to speak in the church." (I Corinthians, 14:34–35)

accusations against her, managing in the process to summarize all English witchlore to date—and to provide local precedents for Salem:

> The evidence against her was, (1) that she was found to have such a malignant touch as many persons (men, women and children) who she stroked or touched with any affection or displeasure, or, etc., were taken with deafness, or vomiting, or other violent pains or sickness; (2) she practicing physic, and her medicines being such things as (by her own confession) were harmless, as aniseed, liquors, etc., yet had extraordinary violent effects; (3) she would use to tell such as would not make use of her physic that they would never be healed, and accordingly their diseases and hurts continued, with relapse against the ordinary course, and beyond the apprehension of all physicians and surgeons; (4) some things which she foretold came to pass accordingly; other things she could tell of (as secret speeches, etc.) which she had not ordinary means to come to the knowledge of; (5) she had (upon search) an apparent teat in her secret parts as fresh as if it had been newly sucked and after it had been scanned, upon a forced search, that was withered, and another began on the opposite side; (6) in the prison, in the clear daylight, there was seen in her arms, sitting on the floor, and her clothes up, etc., a little child, which ran from her into another room, and the officer following it, it was vanished. The like child was seen in two other places, to which she had relation; and one maid that saw it, fell sick upon it, and was cured by the said Margaret, who used means to be employed to that end. Her behavior at her trial was very intemperate, lying notoriously, and railing upon the jury and witnesses, etc., and in the like distemper she died. The same day and hour

she was executed, there was a very great tempest at Connecticut, which blew down many trees, etc.

And then there was Mary Dyer, who went into exile with Anne Hutchinson early in 1638. She returned from Rhode Island to the Bay Colony in the late 1650s, preaching Quakerism.

Her arrival coincided with the passage of new laws outlawing Quakerism. Legislators explained that like the earlier Hutchinsonians, the Quakers "write blasphemous opinions, despising government, and the order of God in church and commonwealth, speaking evil of dignities, reproaching and reviling magistrates and ministers." Quakers were told to get out or be hanged. On June 1, 1660, Mary Dyer was hanged in Boston.

Rapidly, Quakerism, with its special acceptance of women, was equated with witchcraft, practiced mostly by women. For instance, the visiting Englishman John Josselyn wrote in the 1670s: "There be . . . bottle-bellied witches amongst the Quakers."

THE EXAMPLES of Anne Hutchinson, Mary Dyer, and the Quakers continued to haunt the colony's most intellectual witch hunter, Cotton Mather, right up to the end of the century. Writing his own history of New England, the *Magnalia,* he dredged up every insult and insinuation recorded about Anne Hutchinson. Like Governor Winthrop, he saw women as a ruinous influence on their husbands, commenting on Anne Hutchinson and her followers:

'Tis incredible what alienations of mind . . . the Devil raised in the country upon this odd occasion. . . . They began to seduce women into their notions, and by these women, like their first mother [Eve] they soon hooked in their husbands also.

"ALLEGORY"

This mysterious sixteenth century painting, by an anonymous member of the French School of Fontainebleau, depicts a secret meeting of women outdoors in a marshy grove. Entitled only "Allegory," the painting was probably a conversation piece in an elegant French drawing room. Lords and ladies could have passed many pleasant moments musing over its meaning.

The one certainty is that this is a secret meeting of women. The tall, dense fronds provide a perfect hiding place for such female frolicking. The three naked beauties are up to their waists in the pool, suggesting that they are performing a sacred rite of purification. —ECOLE DE FONTAINEBLEAU, XVI C., LOUVRE MUSEUM, PARIS

The colonists had abandoned the Old World weighed down with centuries of frightening tales and superstitions—which they knew well through folklore, literature, and art. In the New World they found themselves surrounded by Indians they called savages, native Americans who were forever practicing ceremonies which struck the colonists as strange and supernatural.

CHAPTER ELEVEN

The "Woeful Decade"

Anne Hutchinson had made a threatening prophecy in the course of her trial. Cotton Mather, as a young Harvard graduate in his twenties, just coming of political age in the 1680s, shivered as he read her warning to Governor Winthrop and the other magistrates back in 1637:

> Therefore, take heed how you proceed against me; for I know that, for this you go about to do to me, God will ruin you, and your posterity, and this whole state.

Mather and his contemporaries in Boston, Salem, and surrounding villages and towns were that "posterity."

A DECADE OF HORRORS began at the end of the colonial-Indian confrontation known as King Philip's War, 1675–1678. Whites justified massacre of natives on grounds that they were pagan agents of the Devil. The newly arrived settlers insisted that even those native Americans who had been converted to Christianity had expelled the Devil from within themselves, allowing Satan to wander at will among innocent colonists. Cotton Mather expressed the idea more succinctly than most of his contemporaries, and related the onslaught of the witches directly to the Indian presence. Introducing *The Wonders of the Invisible World,* his instant history of the Salem trials, composed within a month after their termination, he explains to his reading public at home and back in England:

> The New Englanders are a people of God settled in those which were once the Devil's territories, and it may easily be supposed that the Devil was exceedingly disturbed when he perceived such a people here . . . Twenty have confessed that they have signed unto a book which the Devil showed them, and engaged in this hellish design of bewitching and ruining our land . . . At prodigious witch-meetings the witches have proceeded so far as to concert and consult the methods of rooting out the Christian religion from this country and setting up instead of it perhaps a more gross diabolism than ever the world saw before . . . It may be feared that, in the horrible tempest which is now upon ourselves, the design of the Devil is to sink that happy settlement of Government wherewith Almighty God has graciously inclined their Majesties to favor us.

In 1689, full-scale warfare broke out when the natives found themselves a strong ally, France. The colonists then felt themselves to be in a constant state of siege.

Recalling this terrorized atmosphere, Cotton Mather wrote *Decennium Luctuosum,* the "Woeful Decade," and in one pithy paragraph revealed the Indian connection between witchcraft and life in America:

> The story of the prodigious war made by the spirits of the invisible world upon the people of New England in the year 1692 [the year of the Salem witch trials] hath entertained a great part of the English world with a just astonishment; and I have met with some strange things . . . which have made me often think that this inexpli-

cable war might have some of its origins among the Indians whose chief sagamores are well known unto some of our captives to have been horrid sorcerers and hellish conjurers and such as conversed with demons.

That word "captives" toward the end refers to Mary Rowlandson and Mercy Short. Each in her own way fueled the Salem witch hunt. In a spellbinding book published at Cambridge, Massachusetts, and London, England, back in 1682, Mary Rowlandson told the story of her own captivity —an immediate bestseller on both sides of the Atlantic. She had been wounded and captured in the siege of Lancaster, a tiny frontier settlement thirty-five miles west of Boston, in the course of King Philip's War. Forced to serve as a slave and to march one hundred fifty miles with her captors through snow-covered New England, she was finally ransomed and set free eleven weeks and five days later.

Despite her ordeal, and more suffering than she could bear when her six-year-old daughter Sarah died in her arms, Mary Rowlandson came close to defending her captors for retaliating against the colonists. At the same time, however, she filled her little book with descriptions of mysterious rituals and devil-like monsters. For example, describing her first days among the Indians, she wrote:

> Oh, the roaring, and singing and dancing, and yelling of those black creatures in the night, which made the place a lively resemblance of hell.

Mary Rowlandson returned safely to colonial society, conspicuously respected by the Indians—one gave her a captured Bible and none abused her. The forty-year-old woman assured the world and her readers that never once had the Indians compromised her chastity:

I have been in the midst of those . . . that feared neither God, nor man, nor the Devil, by night and day, alone and in company: sleeping all sorts together, and yet not one of them offered the least abuse of unchastity to me, in word or action.

As for Mercy Short, the other captive to whom Cotton Mather referred when he introduced his tale of New England's "Woeful Decade," she told her story orally—to the Reverend himself. In 1690, just two years before the Salem outbreak, when she was fifteen-years-old, she had been snatched from her home in Salmon Falls, New Hampshire, on the border of Maine. Before her very eyes she saw her father, mother, brother, sister, and other relatives killed. Then, along with three surviving brothers and two sisters, she was forced to march to Canada where she was kept for many long months, till ransomed and taken to Boston as a household servant.

The Devil she described to Rev. Mather as "a short and a black man . . . no taller than an ordinary walking-staff; he was not of a Negro but of a tawny or an Indian color."

THE NEW ENGLAND COUNTRYSIDE, then, was rampant with devils in the shape of Indian men—and with practitioners of the supernatural in the form of Indian women.

The Indians themselves provided further evidence. For example, this "Passamaquoddy Wizard's Chant" sings of beneficent or evil beings that dwell in every rock, tree, and river:

> *I sit and beat the wizard's drum;*
> *And by its mystic sound I call the beasts.*

Another Passamaquoddy chant describes a "demon" that was "even to devils a terror":

I call on the Terrible One,
On the One with the Horns,
I dare him to appear!

It came in all its horrors,
Its eyes were like deep red fire,
Its horns rose sharp and high.

Puritans had always believed that they were the new Chosen People, abandoning a land of sin and oppression (old England) to establish the Promised Land (New England). Now, surrounded by Indians with their heathen ways and pagan gods, Cotton Mather saw the Lord punishing the Puritans for what the Reverend termed their "Indianization"—"swearing, sabbath-breaking, whoring, drunkenness."

Thus, it came as no surprise when the Salem scenario of 1692 opened with the arrest of Tituba, the West Indian slave belonging to Samuel Parris, minister of Salem Farms. She had outraged the Puritans by daring to introduce several young girls to the forbidden art of foretelling the future. Further, she mixed urine with rye to make what she called a witch cake, full of magical properties. And in the dark of the night she gave lessons in chanting and dancing to gain mysterious powers.

When the trials began, several accused witches told of their frightening nightmares about Indians. Sixty-year-old Sarah Osborne, one of the first three arrested and tried, testified:

She was frighted one time in her sleep and either saw or dreamed that she saw a thing like an Indian, all black, which did pinch her in the neck and pulled her by the back part of her head to the door of the house.

A few months later, the Widow Toothaker of Billerica blamed her own suspicious activities on being "troubled with fear about the Indians," adding that she "used to dream of fighting with them." She concluded:

> The Devil appeared to her in the shape of a tawny man and promised to keep her from the Indians . . . if she would serve him . . . She signed [the Devil's book] upon that condition and was to praise him with her whole heart, and 'twas to that appearance she prayed at all times, for he said he was able to deliver her from the Indians. And it was the fear of the Indians that put her upon it.

The stories of Sarah Osborne and the Widow Toothaker, as well as the captivity narratives of Mary Rowlandson and Mercy Short, are representative of countless others. Unfortunately, it was women who suffered most when Indian-colonial relations deteriorated to bloodshed. Left alone and unprotected when husbands went off to attack or to seek help, wives and older daughters would either be killed on the spot by raiding Indians or their French allies, or be taken into captivity as slaves—or live in constant fear of suffering these fates.

IN MANY OTHER WAYS, too, the years Cotton Mather labeled the "Woeful Decade" were particularly hard on women. For example, when Massachusetts degenerated into anarchy—after losing its precious charter of independence and rebelling against royally imposed Governor Edmund Andros in the spring of 1689—two dire consequences followed for women. First, the legislature had no power to enact or enforce taxes to feed or shelter the increasing number of helpless and abandoned widows. Second, the lack of legal authority to mediate disputes resulted in many accusations against women for trespassing on a neighbor's property, or stealing or killing farm animals, or forcing an otherwise unwilling husband to take action on a boundary dispute. Females were especially liable to be blamed because they were always around the house and highly visible when the angry neighbor came to make his claim or protest. In contrast, the husband would be way out at the end of the field; or far away from home fighting Indians, or hunting for meat, or taking care of business in town.

Significantly, eleven of the first twelve accused and examined for witchcraft in Salem were women, in the two months between February 29 and April 21, 1692. And all were members of families involved in long-running land disputes. The single man arrested was John Proctor who entangled himself by vociferously denouncing the proceedings against his wife Elizabeth.

AMAZON GODDESS

Diana was a fierce goddess whose temple at Aricia, near Rome, was a shrine for women. Worshipped by the ancient Amazons, she was transformed by medieval demonology into leader of the witches.

In the painting Diana, goddess of the hunt, moon, and childbirth, stands alone in full-length portrait. She is neither attached to nor dependent on any man. Her only companion is a dog who, with front paws raised, seems ready to pounce at any moment on his prey. Diana stands confidently, the crescent moon ornamenting her hair, looking back for just an instant before she puts an arrow to her bow. —"DIANA, THE HUNTRESS," ECOLE DE FONTAINEBLEAU, XVI C. LOUVRE MUSEUM, PARIS

Men looking for a reason to fear independent women had only to read any of the innumerable myths of Diana which were part of colonial library collections. Diana was also emblazoned in the pages of the New Testament, Acts 19:24–35.

CHAPTER TWELVE

"Contract with the Devil"

Death to anyone caught making a pact with the Devil. This had been the law of the land, according to King James's statute of 1604, long before the Puritan founders of Massachusetts Bay had even dreamed of leaving their English homes for the New World. And now, three generations later, in 1692, the same law, transported intact to British America, governed the trials at Salem.

Salem witch-hunters and judges convinced themselves that women, deliberately excluded from a government based on a covenant with God, would do the next best thing. They would make a pact with the Devil, in order to seize power. As proof of the effectiveness of these demonic contracts, male authorities had only to look at the anarchy, warfare, and economic depression engulfing their colony, which had originally been set up as paradise on earth.

THE FIRST THREE SALEM VILLAGERS condemned for witchcraft were all women—Sarah Good, a beggar scraping along on food and clothing grudgingly handed out by neighbors; Sarah Osborne, a sixty-year-old helpless invalid; and the slave Tituba. Too frequently, they are dismissed by heartless historians as village characters, deserving their fate.

Arrested on Monday, February 29, 1692, the three women

were taken the following morning to the house of Lieutenant Nathaniel Ingersoll, where a makeshift hearing room had been set up. But eager crowds forced the court to move to the Village meetinghouse. The two men chosen to preside, John Hathorne and Jonathan Corwin, were highly respected by the community, but totally ignorant of the law and legal procedure. Nevertheless, they began the official examinations, first questioning Sarah Good.

Sarah Good's hard life was reflected in her face. Seventy years old most observers thought her—somehow forgetting that she had a daughter, Dorcas, who was only five or six.

As a child, Sarah Good had grown up in the comfortable home of her father, the prosperous John Solart, a Wenham innkeeper. Wenham was one of the villages constantly quarreling with Salem Village over boundaries, and whose residents were forever suing and being sued by the inhabitants of Salem Village over land claims. With land titles cancelled by the King's recall of the Old Charter, no earthly solution was at hand.

Neighbors viewed Sarah as the kind of person who naturally attracts misfortune and then takes revenge on everyone and anyone. Life began going downhill for her in 1672 when her father committed suicide, forever disgracing himself and all his descendants in Puritan eyes. Her mother gained control of the Solart estate of £500 and seventy-seven acres of land, quickly remarried, and refused to share the wealth with any of her seven children. Ten years later, in 1682, the seven asked the Massachusetts General Court to reapportion John Solart's legacy, pointing out that Sarah in particular had received only a tiny parcel of property, far less than her due portion.

The court granted Sarah some relief, but even so, bad luck and failure continued to stalk her. First, she married her indentured servant, Daniel Poole, who died soon after, leaving her heavily burdened with his own debts. Then she married again, this time a laborer named William Good. Sued by her first husband's creditors, Sarah was ordered to forfeit some land belatedly turned over from her father's estate. Soon after, hurt by the bad economic times that overwhelmed the colony with inflation and joblessness, Sarah and her second husband sold off the remainder of her legacy and resorted to begging for food and shelter. The low state to which she had fallen bursts through her explanation for staying away from church: "want of clothes."

Following her arrest, she was kept at Ipswich jail, five miles away. Though heavily guarded to and from court each day, she leaped off the horse three different times in unsuccessful attempts to escape. Scorning all authority during her five-day-long interrogation, she screamed at the magistrates and tried to kill herself.

Significantly, even when her activities involve her husband, she is the one who is considered to be demonically inspired, while he recedes into the invisible background. The reasons for this are clear in the records.

First of all, William Good helped himself immeasurably by telling the judges what they most wanted to hear—two different times. Court reporter Ezekiel Cheevers quoted William, in the third person, on March 1, 1692, just one day after his wife's arrest:

> It was here that her husband had said that he was afraid that she either was a witch or would be one very quickly. The worst. [Judge] Hathorne asked him his reason why he said so of her, whether he had ever seen anything by her. He answered no, not in this nature, but it was her bad carriage to him, and indeed, said he, I may say with tears that she is an enemy to all good.

Four days later, William returned to elaborate:

William Good sayeth that the night before his said wife was examined, he saw a wart or tit a little below her right shoulder which he never saw before.

This of course referred to the telltale witch's tit, which the Devil or a familiar sucked. Any birthmark or scar would do to prove its owner a witch beyond question.

In other testimony, both Sarah and William Good are equally involved. But all vituperation is directed at Sarah alone. For example, there is the deposition of Samuel Abbey and his wife Mary, described as being forty-five and thirty-eight respectively, and residents of Salem Village:

About this time three years past, William Good and his wife Sarah Good being destitute of a house to dwell in, these deponents out of charity, they being poor, let them live in theirs some time until that the said Sarah Good was of so turbulent a spirit, spiteful and so maliciously bent that these deponents could not suffer her to live in their house any longer and was forced for quietness sake to turn the said Sarah with her husband out of their house ever since, which is about two and a half years ago.

The said Sarah Good hath carried it very spitefully and maliciously towards them. The winter following after the said Sarah was gone from our house, we began to lose . . . seventeen head of cattle within this two years besides sheep and hogs, and both do believe they died by witchcraft.

Some of the village contempt for Sarah's habits of begging and pipe-smoking, along with awe for her powers for inflicting evil, comes through in the testimony of twenty-one-year-old Henry Herrick who dredged up an old recollection:

Last March was two years that Sarah Good came to his father's house and desired to lodge there. His father forbade it and she went away grumbling. My father bade us follow her and see that she went away clear, lest she should lie in the barn, and by the smoking of her pipe should fire the barn. [Henry and one of his friends] seeing her make a stop near the barn, bade her be gone . . . to which she replied that then it should cost his father Zachariah Herrick one or two of the best cows which he had . . . Since that time several of their cattle have been set loose in a strange manner.

Recurring smallpox epidemics brought every family death and fear. Thus Sarah and Thomas Gadge, both about forty years old, refused food or clothing to Sarah Good, barring her from their house, "afraid she had been with them that had smallpox." Sarah Good reacted strongly, according to Sarah Gadge:

She fell to muttering and scolding extremely and so told said Gadge if she would not let her in she should give her something . . . And the next morning . . . one of said Gadge's cows died in a sudden terrible and strange unusual manner so that some of the neighbors and [Gadge] did think it to be done by witchcraft.

Thomas Gadge corroborated his wife's testimony:

He had a cow who died about the time above mentioned, and though he and some neighbors opened the cow yet they could find no natural cause of said cow's death.

Undaunted—and in sharp contrast to her husband—Sarah Good fought the judges almost every step of the way. At her first examination on March 1, 1692, the morning after her arrest, she denied all accusations.

Again and again Judge Hathorne—ancestor of Salem's great nineteenth century novelist, Nathaniel Hawthorne—returned to the Devil's pact. The question and the answer were always the same:

Have you made no contract with the Devil?
No.

Then Judge Hathorne ordered several young girls present at the hearing to look at Sarah Good "and see if this were the person who had hurt them." They looked and immediately fell into fits. (The recorder used "H" to indicate Judge Hathorne's questions and "G" for Sarah Good's answers:)

(H) Sarah Good, do you not see now what you have done? Why do you not tell us the truth. Why do you thus torment these poor children?
(G) I do not torment them.
(H) Who do you employ then?
(G) I employ nobody. I scorn it.
(H) How came they thus tormented?
(G) What do I know you bring others here and now you charge me with it?

By the end of her first examination, Sarah Good's fright and exhaustion produced an emotional outburst. When the Judge tried to question her on religion, this dialogue occurred:

(H) Who do you serve?
(G) I serve God.
(H) What God do you serve?

(G) The God that made heaven and earth. [Here the recorder switched, without pause, from Sarah Good's words to his own comments:] Her answers were in a very wicked, spiteful manner, reflecting and retorting against the authority with base and abusive words and many lies.

For four and a half tortured months she languished in prison, till her hanging on July 19.

SARAH OSBORNE was the second to face examination by the makeshift court. Like Sarah Good, she was questioned on a pact with the Devil and accused of hurting the children, who obligingly fell into fits. Another similarity in the testimony of the two women was their admission of failure to attend church, Sarah Good for lack of clothes and Sarah Osborne because she was bedridden. The significant new element in Goody Osborne's testimony was her fear of Indian attack.

Sarah Osborne's story is that of a wife victimized by her dead husband's enemies. She had first come to the newly formed Salem Village in 1662 as the bride of Robert Prince, owner of a 150-acre farm. Prosperous and politically active, Robert Prince added to his holdings, buying land on the disputed Salem Village-Topsfield boundary and signed petition after petition to guarantee the Village's independence of the parent Salem Town. Like many of his fellow Villagers, he wanted no tax obligations or militia duty connected with Salem Town and refused to help pay for a new meetinghouse there.

Outspoken and conspicuous in life, he attempted to rule his roost after death by stipulating in his will that his wife turn over his property to their two sons, six-year-old James and two-year-old Joseph when they came of age. Sarah was to handle the land in trust, but supervised by Prince's neighbors, who were also his in-laws, Thomas and John Putnam.

Sometime after her husband's death in 1682, Sarah Prince married her indentured servant Alexander Osborne. Together they attempted to change the will of her first husband, so that they might have full control over his property.

Now enter the Putnams, those neighbors and in-laws of the deceased husband, Robert Prince. They were the men conspicuously behind the core group of hysterical females naming and testifying against accused witches. In fact, Thomas Putnam kept such a careful eye on the proceedings that when the judges began showing signs of lenience by mid-April, he fired off a letter warning them about "high and dreadful things" yet to come.

In turn, the Putnams were closely allied with thirty-nine-year-old Samuel Parris, the beleaguered minister of Salem Village, who had caused the inhabitants to split into two warring factions: haters and supporters. A Harvard dropout and failed trader in Barbados, the Reverend had drifted to Salem Village, a quarreling community unable to agree on an acceptable minister. The Rev. Parris's price for bringing order out of chaos was to establish himself as a latter day lord of the manor who dictated all community actions and received all money and property demanded. Anyone crossing him or his supporters was obviously allied with the Devil. Hence the arrest of Sarah Osborne as a witch. Though bedridden for years, she was accused by Tituba's young followers of being present "at the general meeting of the witches in the field near Mr. Parris's house."

Following six days of questioning, she was thrown into prison. There she remained for nine weeks and two days, from March 7 to May 10, 1692, when she died—privately in her dirt-floored cell rather than publicly on the gallows.

THE EXAMINATIONS came full circle when Tituba—the exotic, complete outsider who had been the first arrested—was dragged to an official hearing as the third defendant on March 1.

Uneducated and torn from her Caribbean homeland to live in the unfamiliar environment of Salem Village, she found the people, the climate, and the religion totally incomprehensible. Besides, she could barely understand the English lan-

Sarah Good and Sarah Osborne, the first two women cried out on by Tituba and her young charges, fit in well with the old English stereotype of witches.

Illustration from a chapbook circulated in late sixteenth century England, before the Puritans embarked for the New World. —COURTESY BRITISH LIBRARY

guage used all around her. To her young charges, nine-year-old Elizabeth Parris and eleven-year-old Abigail Williams, the half-black, half-Indian Tituba demonstrated—with actions rather than words—the voodoo magic that had been part of her life in Barbados. These children were the daughter and niece respectively of Tituba's owner, Samuel Parris, the Village minister. In turn, the girls shared their exciting but forbidden knowledge with their friends: sickly, twelve-year-old Ann Putnam, daughter of Thomas Putnam, clerk of the parish;

seventeen-year-old Mercy Lewis, a servant in the Putnam household; and seventeen-year-old Mary Walcott, daughter of Jonathan Walcott, parish deacon.

Legend has it that the young girls invited others to join their charmed circle, usually at the Parris home, where they read palms and told fortunes, performed weird dances, and uttered strange chants. This went on for about two months, from December, 1691, till February, 1692, when some of the adults discovered the antics and raised questions about the strange goings-on. The girls took the time-honored way out: they blamed witches. Pressed to name names, they had come up first with Tituba, who was nearest and most obvious, and then went further afield, naming Sarah Good and Sarah Osborne. Accusations against the two Sarahs fit in perfectly with the village attitude that they were nuisances, in everybody's way.

Tituba's testimony was peppered with age-old folklore, though the fact that she could speak very little English makes it possible that the judges or the court reporter actually put the words in her mouth.

For example, the sixty-year-old slave is recorded several times as describing her ride through the air. Here is a typical excerpt:

(Hathorne) How did you go?
(Tituba) We ride upon sticks and are there presently.
(Hathorne) Do you go through the trees or over them?
(Tituba) We see nothing but are there presently.

In two different examinations, Tituba refers to child-killing. First, she testifies:

[Sarah] Good tells her she must kill somebody with a knife and would have had her kill Thomas Putnam's child last night.

Later, she gives a slightly different version of the same tale:

There was an appearance that said kill the children and if I would not go on hurting the children they would do worse to me.

This "appearance" comes to her in the form of various familiars, to do the Devil's work:

Sometimes it is like a hog, and sometimes like a great dog, . . . [or] a man with a yellow bird . . . [or] two rats, a red rat and a black rat.

Over and over, Tituba's attention and tales focus on Sarah Good:

Good came to her last night when her master was at prayer and would not let her hear. Hath one yellow bird and stopped her ears in prayer time. The yellow bird hath been seen by the children and Tituba saw it suck Good between the forefinger and long finger upon the right hand . . . Saw Good have a cat besides the bird, and a thing all over hairy.

The pact with the Devil was part of Tituba's testimony against Sarah Good:

Saw Good's name in the book and the Devil told her they [presumably the familiars she had described as accompanying Sarah] made the marks.

Sarah Osborne fared no better in Tituba's testimony:

She had a thing with a head like a woman, with two legs, and wings. Abigail Williams that lives with her

Uncle Parris said that she did see the same creature, and it turned into the shape of Goody Osborne.

When Judge Hathorne questioned Tituba about anything else she may have seen accompanying Goody Osborne, she was recorded as responding obediently:

> Another thing, hairy, it goes upright like a man. It hath only two legs.

Tituba's testimony was highly effective sensationalism. And she was backed up by several of the young girls—as well as by five-or-six-year-old Dorcas Good, whose deposition against her own mother childishly promised three birds as familiars, but stopped after describing only two:

> She had three birds, one black, one yellow, and that these birds hurt the children and afflicted persons.

The treatment meted out to little Dorcas and to Tituba reveals some discouraging sidelights about Salem procedure. The child, tainted by being the daughter of a witch, was thrown into prison with her mother, despite having given supporting testimony. Starved, confined for many months, and probably chained along with other witches, she was spared the gallows, but driven mad for the rest of her life.

As for Tituba, she received no special consideration for her helpful confession or for her testimony against others. Instead, she was viewed as a particularly troublesome ringleader, and imprisoned for eighteen months, then sold to pay her jail costs. (In the seventeenth century, these costs were always charged to the prisoner, the next of kin, or the guardian.)

Throwing a child into the fire. An illustration of an old folk theme. From the *Compendium Maleficarum* (Compilation of Witchcraft) by Francesco-Maria Guazzo, 1608.

CHAPTER THIRTEEN

"An Evil Hand"

Increasingly, bloody quarreling between neighbors made witches out of wives, and perverted solemn courtrooms into supernatural dens of iniquity. Testimony took on the aura of an eerie folktale, with the accused witch forced into the role of wicked queen.

TITUBA AND THE CHILDREN next cried out on sixty-year-old Martha Corey. She was the third wife of Giles Corey, at eighty-one the owner of one hundred extremely valuable acres of land near the Ipswich River. He had spent a lifetime quarreling with neighbors, making trouble in and out of court. But it was Martha who was questioned about witchcraft at the Corey home on Saturday March 12, arrested one week later on March 19, examined at court on Monday March 21, convicted, and slapped into Boston prison till her hanging on Thursday, September 22.

Maybe because the act of marrying a witch made a husband open to suspicion, Giles testified against Martha in late March. But he failed to save himself and was similarly arrested on April 18. Five months later, on September 19, refusing to recognize the jurisdiction of the court, he was pressed to death by court officers who tried to make him confess to witchcraft by laying one heavy boulder after another on his aged chest. Historians have had a high old time debating whether English law enabled Giles Corey to preserve his property for his children by taking this action to avoid conviction.

In contrast to Giles's behavior, Martha never denounced her husband—or anyone else in the course of her examination. In fact, the court record notes her refusal "to help to find out witches." Openly contemptuous of the proceedings, she had deliberately refrained from following the crowds to hear and watch the examinations of Tituba and the two Sarahs. Worse, though only a woman, she had tried—unsuccessfully—to impose her ideas on her husband by removing the saddle from his horse to keep him at home too.

From the very beginning she insulted her inquisitors. Ezekiel Cheevers and Edward Putnam who had first questioned her at home reported that she had showed insufficient respect:

> She made little answer, . . . but seemed to smile. She told us that she did not think there were any witches.

In the courtroom she behaved no better, rebutting the judges at every turn. For example:

> Do you not believe there are witches in the country?
> I do not know that there are any.
> Do not you know that Tituba confessed it?
> I did not hear her speak.

Asked whether she had covenanted with the Devil or promised him ten years of service, she laughed in the judges' faces. And when Hathorne questioned her about the young girls' collective accusations that she had a yellow bird with her for a familiar, and that they saw a man whispering in her ear, she again laughed, adding: "We must not believe all that these distracted children say."

A deeply religious woman, she embarrassed the magistrates

by calling on God for help, thus casting doubt on their methods:

> The Lord open the eyes of the magistrates and ministers: the Lord show his power to discover the guilty.

In his most sarcastic manner, Hathorne later tried to use these words against her, though omitting the Lord in his paraphrase:

> Did you not say you would open our eyes? Why do you not?

To the question, "What book is that you would have these children write in?" she responded in words that produce ringing tones when read aloud:

> What book? Where should I have a book? I showed them none, nor have none, nor brought none.

Martha Corey was obviously an articulate, strong-willed woman who fought every accusation made by the court or by hostile witnesses. Without doubt, however, such a woman, almost a full generation younger than her husband, would have been conspicuous in the management of family affairs—and would thereby have put herself on the firing line.

AT 8:00 A.M. ON THURSDAY, MARCH 24, Marshal George Herrick arrested Rebecca Nurse. She was the fourth witch to be accused by Tituba and the children.

Scandalously, the children had been pressed into service as fronts for angered men. The complaint was sworn out by Edward and Jonathan Putnam, sons of wealthy John Putnam and nephews of Nathaniel Putnam, the Reverend Parris's staunchest ally. And as for Rebecca Nurse, she was seventy-one-years-old and so sick that she almost never left her bed. In addition, she was almost completely deaf. Chained in prison for more than two months, her sick body literally decaying, she was acquitted at her trial on June 2—only to have the case reopened when the coterie of young girls performed their fits so dramatically that the judges, on June 28, confronted the old woman with self-confessed witch Deliverance Hobbs of Topsfield and her daughter Abigail.

"What, do these persons give evidence against me now? They used to come among us," Rebecca Nurse cried out.

Her deafness prevented her from hearing the court's interpretation that this was a confession of associating with other witches. It was already too late when she finally understood enough to protest that she knew the Hobbses as fellow prisoners, not as witches.

The recently appointed royal governor, Sir William Phipps, reading over the record of her two hearings, as well as the many petitions pleading for her release, came close to reprieving her. At the last minute, however, he lost courage and let her go to the gallows on July 19.

Once arrested, then, there was no escape for Rebecca Nurse. But why was she singled out in the first place?

First, there was a hoary tale that her mother had been a witch. It was soberly repeated in the courtroom and seriously accepted by the judges. Without question, the daughter of a witch was always a witch herself. The fact that Rebecca's sisters, Sarah Cloyce and Mary Easty, were subsequently tried and convicted for witchcraft, bears out this point.

Here the star witness was Ann Putnam, Sr., thirty-year-old wife of the powerful Nathaniel Putnam. A once intelligent, now half-demented woman—she had lost several of her own children and had seen her beloved sister Mary Bailey die after the ordeal of three separate stillbirths—Ann, Sr. used the tale of the mother witch to the hilt:

Rebecca Nurse . . . and her sister Cloyce . . . had killed young John Putnam's child because young John Putnam had said that it was no wonder they were witches for their mother was so before them, and because they could not avenge themselves on him they killed his child. And immediately there did appear to me . . . my own sister Bailey and three of her children in winding sheets, and told me that Goody Nurse had murdered them.

Young John Putnam and his wife Hannah themselves took the stand against Rebecca Nurse. The poignancy of the parents' grief must have affected every listener with similar fear and sorrow:

Our child which died about the middle of April, 1692, was as well and as thriving a child as most till it was about eight weeks old. But awhile after that, I, the said John Putnam, had reported something which I had heard concerning the mother of Rebecca Nurse, Mary Easty, and Sarah Cloyce . . . Quickly after this our poor young child was taken about midnight with strange and violent fits which did most grievously frighten us . . . where-upon we sent for our mother Putnam in the night. Immediately as soon as she came and saw our child she told us that she feared there was an evil hand upon it. And also as fast as possibly could be we got a doctor to it, but all he did give it could do it no good, but it continued in strange and violent fits for about two days and two nights, and then departed this life by a cruel and violent death, being enough to pierce a stony heart, for to the best of our understanding it was near five hours a-dying.

This kind of testimony was highly effective for convicting Rebecca Nurse. Even so, it hardly explains (1) her arrest in the first place, (2) the court's overturning its own early finding of innocence, (3) the new governor's hesitation to grant a reprieve.

Fortunately, the injustice of her execution has prompted three centuries of research on her life, down to the most minute details.

Her family tree provides a basic clue. Before marriage she was a member of the Towne family living in Topsfield. This was a town that highlighted all the drawbacks of a colony with no government in charge for three years. Until Governor Phipps finally arrived with a new charter on May 14, 1692, vague boundaries that overlapped private farms as well as whole villages were settled not by mutual agreement, but by weapons and violence. Thus the Towne family on the Topsfield side claimed land rights against their neighbors, the Putnams, on the other side of the border in Salem Village.

The feud between the Putnams and the Townes reached its murderous climax in court when Ann Putnam, Sr., and her allies denounced first Rebecca Towne Nurse and then her sisters, Mary Towne Easty and Sarah Towne Cloyce.

Another problem for Rebecca Nurse was her strong loyalty to her husband Francis. This brought her the enmity of the influential Village minister, Samuel Parris. Several years before, Francis Nurse had openly refused to support the Reverend Parris's claim to ownership of the Salem Village parsonage and the land surrounding it. Unforgiving and unforgetting, the Reverend—half hiding behind the young girls who first came to public attention at his house—now found it easier to take revenge on the sick, helpless wife than on the still strapping-and-scrapping husband.

However, at least one piece of testimony seems to indicate that in her better days Rebecca Nurse had been no easy target. The widow Sarah Holton recalled:

> About this time three years, my dear and loving husband Benjamin Holton, now deceased, was as well as ever

I knew him in my life, till one Saturday morning that Rebecca Nurse who now stands charged with witchcraft came to our house and fell a-railing at him because our pigs got into her field. Though our pigs were sufficiently yoked and their fence was down in several places, yet all we could say to her could no ways pacify her, but she continued railing and scolding a great while together, calling to her son Benjamin Nurse to go and get a gun and kill our pigs and let none of them go out of the field.

Of course, this gives only one side of the story. Rebecca Nurse's side, easy to construe, provides the strongest possible indication of why a woman—Rebecca Nurse in this particular instance—would get into trouble and subsequently be singled out as a witch. As the wife, she had complete responsibility for the household garden, principal source of the family food supply. Allowing a neighbor's straying pigs to destroy the fruits of her exhausting labor would threaten her family's sustenance. (Besides the parents, Rebecca and Francis, there were eight children, four daughters and four sons.) In contrast, her husband, though ultimately affected by a porcine invasion, would be working far out of sight.

In the end, the court was forced to rely heavily on spectral evidence to convict Rebecca Nurse. A typical witness was Abigail Williams, niece of Rev. Samuel Parris, who described eleven different days in the months of March, April, and May when she had "been exceedingly perplexed with the apparition of Rebecca Nurse of Salem Village":

By which apparition she had been pulled violently and often pinched and almost choked and tempted sometimes to leap into the fire and sometimes to subscribe a book the said apparition brought, and also she sayeth that she has seen this apparition at a sacrament sitting next to the

In a plea for her life, submitted to the court, Rebecca Nurse indicated her approval with a sign beside "hir mark."— PHOTOGRAPH BY NANCY BAER, WITH THE KIND COOPERATION OF THE SALEM SUPERIOR COURT.

man with a high crowned hat at the upper end of the table and further sayeth that said apparition has sometimes confessed to her the said Abigail its guilt in committing several murders together with her sister Cloyce.

THAT SAME TUESDAY, JULY 19, when Rebecca Nurse climbed the ladder to be "turned off" at the gallows, four other women were similarly hanged. They were Elizabeth How and Sarah Wildes, both from Topsfield, Susannah Martin of Amesbury, and Sarah Good whose story was told in Chapter Twelve.

Elizabeth and James How, married for thirty-four years, lived with their two daughters on the Topsfield-Ipswich border, a boundary line hotly contested by the two villages, each of which claimed the right to tax its residents. All private landowners had to make new claims under the charter, which arrived in mid-May, 1692. This is when Elizabeth How's troubles began. In fact, the charter arrived on May 14, and she was arrested on May 29.

Since James How was blind, his wife would have had charge of managing their farm. Her angry neighbors, the Perleys, were key witnesses at her trial. Set in testimony that sounds like the encounter between Hansel and Gretel and the old witch, Sam Perley nonchalantly dropped a hint of their real cause of anger almost at the beginning (pertinent words italicized):

We having a daughter about ten years of age being in a sorrowful condition, *this being soon after a falling out that had been between James How and his wife and myself,* our daughter told us that it was James How's wife that afflicted her both night and day sometimes complaining of being pricked with pins and sometimes falling down into dreadful fits . . . One day we went to several doctors and they told us that [our daughter] was under an evil hand. Our daughter told us that when she came near the fire or water this witch pulls me in.

The daughter, named Hannah, had an aunt and uncle, Timothy and Deborah Perley, who picked up where the father had left off, quoting the young girl as screaming: "There's that woman. She goes into the oven and out again." Then Deborah Perley related that young Hannah "fell into a dreadful fit, and when I have asked her when she said 'that woman' what woman she meant, she told me James How's wife."

SARAH WILDES, wife of farmer John Wildes, and also a resident of embattled Topsfield, was similarly sentenced on June 29 to be hanged on July 19. Her family was heavily involved in the feud between Topsfield and Salem Village, and she herself was very protective of family property, never allowing neighbors to trespass or to borrow farm implements without express permission.

Unhappily, these are all the facts known about Sarah Wildes. However, they are sufficient to point strongly to the reasons for her persecution—reasons that are all-but-identical with those in the superlatively recorded case of Rebecca Nurse, or the fairly well-recorded case of Elizabeth How.

At the trial of the widowed Susannah Martin of Amesbury, there were at least fifteen adult males among the hostile witnesses. In her case, the records show strong hints as to the real cause of conflict.

When her husband was still alive, Susannah Martin had been tried and found guilty of witchcraft. Thus her past was readily available to haunt her. Now, amid the usual screaming interruptions of the young girls—who saw her hanging from a ceiling beam, or entertaining the Devil in court, or biting someone—a former neighbor, forty-five-year old John Kimball, dredged up an old story dating back to her first trial, twenty-three years before. He remembered how Susannah Martin had insisted that he live up to his part of the bargain whereby he would pay cash or goods in return for land owned by her husband George Martin. When Kimball offered the Martins three cows, but not two others which he particularly wanted to keep, "Martin himself was satisfied," but not his wife who threatened that if they would not part with one of the two cows, "she will never do you any more good." And sure enough, a month later that very cow lay dead in the yard, though careful examination revealed no reason. "And in a little while after, another cow died, and then an ox, and then other cattle to the value of £30 that spring." In other words, anger over a property dispute combined with the chance deaths of several farm animals to mark Susannah Martin as a witch.

To George Corwine Gentlm High Sheriff of ye County of Esex Greeting

Whereas Sarah Good Wife of William Good of Salem Village Rebecka Nurse wife of Francis Nurse of Salem Village Susanna Martin of Amesbury Widow Elizabeth How wife of James How of Ipswich Sarah Wild Wife of John Wild of Topsfield all of ye County of Essex in their Majties Province of ye Massachusets Bay in Newengland Att a Court of Oyer & terminer held by Adjournment for Our Soueraign Lord & Lady King William & Queen Mary for ye Said County of Essex at Salem in ye sd County One ye 29th day of June were seuerally araign'd On Seuerall Indictments for ye horrible Crime of Witchcraft by them practised & Comitted On Seuerall persons and pleading not guilty did for thier Tryall put themselues On God & thier Countrey whereupon they were Each of them found & brought in Guilty by ye Jury that passed On them according to thier respectiue Indictmts and Sentence of death did then pass vpon them as the Law directs Execution whereof yet remains to be done:

These are Therefore in thier Majties names William & Mary now King & Queen over England &c: to Will & Comand you that vpon Tuesday next being ye 19th day of this Instant July between ye houres of Eight & tweluw in ye forenoon ye same day you Safely conduct ye sd Sarah Good Rebecka Nurse Susanna Martin Elizabeth How & Sarah Wild from thier Majties Goal in Salem afored to ye place of Execution & there Cause them & Euery of them to be hanged by ye Neck vntill they be dead and of ye doeings herein make return to ye Clerke of ye Said Court & this precept and hereof you are not to fail at your perill and this Shall be your Sufficient Warrant Giuen vnder my hand & Seale at Boston the 12th day of July in ye fourth yeare of ye Reign of Our Soueraign Lord & Lady Wm & Mary King & Queen &c: Wm Stoughton.
Anoqz Domi. 1692.

PERSONAL NOTE

No matter how many times I read the cold,
three-hundred-year-old words on this tattered death warrant, my
cast-iron stomach dissolves into waves of sick nausea:

To George Corwin, High Sheriff of the County of Essex,
Greeting:
   Whereas Sarah Good, . . . Rebecca Nurse, . . .
Susannah Martin, . . . Elizabeth How, . . . Sarah
Wildes, . . . all of the County of Essex . . . for the
horrible crime of committing witchcraft by them brought
in and found guilty . . . sentence of death did then pass
upon them as the law directs execution whereof yet remains
to be done.
   . . . On Tuesday next being the 19th day of . . . July
between the hours of eight and . . . forenoon of the same
day you safely conduct [them] to be hanged by the necks
until they be dead. . . .
                    [Signed] William Stoughton [Chief Magistrate]

Salem July: 19: 1692

I caused ye within mentioned persons to be Executed according to ye tenour of ye within Warrant

George Corwin Sh

Legalistically, workmanlike, the reverse side of the warrant duly reports:

Salem, July 19th, 1692:

I caused the within mentioned persons to be executed according to the tenor of the warrant.

[Signed] George Corwin, Sheriff

I had no advance warning that I would run into this document. For years scholars have been assuring themselves and each other that only a single death warrant for witchcraft execution in 1692 remained, that of Bridget Bishop, carefully preserved under glass in Salem Superior Court. Charles W. Upham had made this pronouncement in his classic two-volume study, *Salem Witchcraft,* first published in 1867 and still being reissued (see vol. II, page 266).

Completely by chance, combing the card catalogue listings under "Salem" at the Department of Rare Books and Manuscripts of the Boston Public Library, I found reference to the death warrant pictured here. Now authenticated as original by the Department, it was purchased without fanfare in 1939.

In a quiet corner of the room, I was allowed to read and touch this piece of paper that brought death to five women. Part of the blood-red official wax seal remains near the top left. Somehow, even the discrepancy between the warrant and the court record for Elizabeth How—in the warrant she is described as a resident of Ipswich, in the court record she is called a resident of Topsfield—heightens the drama of death amid the hopelessness of anarchy and chaos.

The disappearance of so many official documents, a further indication of rampant confusion, has made it difficult for history to restore individual identity and dignity to witch-hunt victims. I salute the memory of each victim.

S.R.W.

CIRCE

Circe was a witch, a goddess of beasts, an enchantress. In Homer's *Odyssey* she performed her sorcery through magical foods and irresistible hospitality. She was the prototype of the witch who as innkeeper could transform food into poison and men into beasts. First she lured members of the crew of Odysseus (called Ulysses by the Romans) who had just docked at her island, attracted by her siren song. When they came close enough to her house, she invited them to enter. She also asked Ulysses, captain of the ship, to come in:

On thrones she seated them, and lounging chairs, while she prepared a meal of cheese and barley and amber mixed with Pramnian wine, adding her own vile pinch, to make them lose desire or thought of our dear fatherland. Scarce had they drunk when she flew after them with her long stick and shut them in a pigsty—bodies, voices, heads, and bristles, all swinish now, though minds were still unchanged.—*Odyssey*, BOOK 10. HOMER, SOMETIME BEFORE 700 B.C.

In the painting "Odysseus and Circe," Bartolomeus Spranger (Flemish, 1546–1625) portrays Circe clinging desperately to Odysseus, pleading with him to stay with her. This is part of the episode of the *Odyssey* Homer entitled "The Grace of the Witch." Here, Odysseus advises Circe that he is wise to her evil powers and knows that she has turned most of his crew to swine (symbolizing sensuality and earthiness).—PHOTO COURTESY KUNSTHISTORISCHEN MUSEUM, VIENNA

CHAPTER FOURTEEN

"Queen of Hell"

At a time of gloom nursed by superstition, Bridget Bishop of Salem Town was a highly suspicious character, a woman who ran an alehouse in order to support herself, her children, and her husband. At her tavern she served cider and cheese to roisterous boys and men. Cider, when it turned, could destroy a man, putting him into a drunken stupor, and cheese with its queer green mold might poison him.*

Thus Bridget Bishop had to battle ancient folk belief, passed down through the ages and shaped to New World specifications. For example, Michael Wigglesworth, Puritan minister and poet of Malden, harked back through the centuries as he translated hell, fire, and brimstone into rhyming verses, and

---

* A much quoted passage written by St. Augustine (354–430 A.D.), repeated also in Thomas Heywood's mid-seventeenth century *General History of Women*, described evil perpetrated by innkeepers:

[Innkeepers] put such confections into a kind of cheese they made that all such travellers as guested with them and ate thereof were presently metamorphosed into laboring beasts, as horses, asses, oxen, which they employed either in drawing or bearing of burdens, or else let them out for hackneys to gain profit by their hire, and when their work was done and they had made of them what benefit they could, they restored them to their pristine shape.

bracketed witches with alehouse keepers. He described a group of principal troublemakers in his descriptively titled work, first published in 1662 and still going strong in 1692, *The Day of Doom, or a Poetical Description of the Great and Last Judgment:*

> *False-witness bearers, and self-forswearers, Murd'rers and men of blood,*
> *Witches, enchanters, and ale housekeepers, beyond count there stood . . .*

The 1692 trial of Bridget Bishop, now well into her sixties or maybe even her seventies, was by no means her first brush with the law or with witchcraft. Arrested and punished long before, in 1652, for lying and stealing Indian corn, she was examined as a witch in 1680, but released. In 1692, however, her luck ran out. On June 2, 1692, exactly three weeks after the arrival of the new governor, she was tried for witchcraft, and on June 10, she became the very first to be hanged as a witch in Salem.

The confusion of early hearings at Salem had resulted in jails overflowing with accused witches. Accordingly, almost the first action of the new royal governor, Sir William Phipps, was to set up a court of Oyer and Terminer—consisting of the deputy governor as well as four highly respected magistrates from Boston, three from Salem, and one from Haverhill—to "hear and decide" the fate of these prisoners. (In this attempt to organize the trials into some semblance of legal procedure, the local affair in Salem turned into a colony-wide responsibility.) The first session was the one held on June 2, which produced the swift conviction and condemnation of Bridget Bishop.* And at the end of the month, in the chaotic haste to

---

* One of the magistrates, Nathaniel Saltonstall of Haverhill, refused to participate in further trials following the case of Bridget Bishop. In a letter to his friend, Boston merchant Thomas Brattle, he explained that he was "very much dissatisfied with the proceedings of it."

clear the jails to make room for more witches, the examinations of the next five women resulted in setting July 19 as the date for their hanging.

But the supposedly well-greased machinery of the new court brought no rhyme or reason to the dates set for trial or for execution. The first arrested were not necessarily the first tried. And the first convicted were not necessarily the first hanged.

Elizabeth Proctor, who, like Bridget Bishop, ran a tavern, was arrested a week earlier than Bridget Bishop. John Proctor (currently on his way to becoming a twentieth century folk hero, thanks to Arthur Miller's much produced play of 1952, *The Crucible*) was arrested the day after his pregnant wife. Defiantly, he had followed her to court to protest and to gain her release. Although John Proctor's arrest came six days before that of Bridget Bishop, he went to the gallows on August 19, whereas Bridget was hanged on June 10. The imprisoned Elizabeth Proctor was allowed to "plead her belly" (in the descriptive vernacular of the time), and because the last hangings had occurred several months before the birth she eventually was released. However, the estate of her husband was confiscated to pay for the couple's jail costs, so that she and her eleven children suffered a life of starvation and abject poverty.

Hanged along with John Proctor on August 19 was Martha Carrier of Andover, who had been arrested some six weeks after him, on May 28. Forty-years-old and the mother of four, she was forced to listen to the parroting testimony given by her eight-year-old daughter Sarah and eighteen-year-old Richard. Both called her witch and told of her efforts to convert them.

The crux of the case against Martha Carrier was her own poetically expressed determination to "stick as close to Benjamin Abbott as the bark stuck to a tree" to prevent him from occupying land granted to him by the town of Andover. At the trial, Benjamin Abbott and his wife testified against

Martha and were helped along by the now-regular routine of the young girls. In despair and disgust, Martha cried out to the magistrates: "It is a shameful thing that you should mind these folks that are out of their minds." Then she turned to denounce her accusers: "You lie. I am wronged."

Yet the Bay Colony's leading intellectual, Cotton Mather, still the power behind the scenes though he never attended any of the trials, had nothing but contempt for Martha Carrier. In his instant history of the Salem proceedings circulated late in 1692, he wrote:

> This rampant hag was the person of whom the confessions of the witches, and of her own children among the rest, agreed that the Devil had promised her that she should be queen of Hell.

THESE "CONFESSIONS OF WITCHES" to which Cotton Mather referred deserve special skepticism. The Reverend had written to Maj. John Richards of Boston, one of the magistrates of the Court of Oyer and Terminer, that he himself was "far from

From a seventeenth century English witchcraft tract.—COURTESY BRITISH LIBRARY

urging the un-English method of torture" in order to obtain confessions.

But this high-sounding statement has to be contrasted with the reality described by Capt. Nathaniel Cary of Charlestown who saved his wife, already accused and awaiting trial, by seizing her from Cambridge jail at night and fleeing with her first to Rhode Island, then to New York. Elizabeth Cary, her husband wrote at the time of her pretrial hearing,

> was forced to stand with her arms stretched out. I requested that I might hold one of her hands, but it was denied me. Then she desired me to wipe the tears from her eyes, and the sweat from her face, which I did; then she desired she might lean herself on me, saying that she should faint. Judge Hathorne replied she had strength enough to torment these persons, and she should have strength enough to stand. I speaking something against their cruel proceedings, they commanded me to be silent, or else I should be turned out of the room.

Nathaniel Cary went on to describe his wife's first night in jail:

> The jailer put irons on her legs . . . The weight of them was about eight pounds. These irons and her other afflictions soon brought her into convulsion fits, so that I thought she would have died that night. I sent to entreat that the irons might be taken off, but all entreaties were in vain.

A letter from John Proctor, found among the Salem records, corroborates Nathaniel Cary's words. John Proctor wrote that his own son, William, "because he would not confess that he was guilty when he was innocent, they tied him neck and heels, till the blood gushed out of his nose."

So much for the value of confessions. Or their usefulness to history for that matter. In court they soon degenerated into a meaningless, memorized rite, everyone using almost the same words. Perversely, those who confessed to witchcraft, the presumed downfall of any society, went free; whereas the accused who denied they were witches were usually executed.

Should any of the carefully learned words and phrases be forgotten, the judges had no hesitation in leading the witness. For example, Abigail Hobbs of Topsfield who had the reputation of being a wild teenager—she wandered in the fields and woods alone at night—was thrown into Salem jail where this interrogation took place:

Where did you stick the thorns?
I do not know.
Was it about the middle of her body?
Yes, and I stuck it right in.

This is the same Abigail Hobbs who at court on June 1, 1692, added still another presence to local witches' meetings— the Devil in the shape of a man well known and intensely disliked by many in the community. He was forty-year-old George Burroughs, the former minister of Salem Village who had moved some fifty miles north to Maine. Unluckily for him, his former servant was one of the hysterical young girls—seventeen-year-old Mercy Lewis—now a servant in the household of Thomas Putnam, a powerful witch-hunter and supporter of Rev. Samuel Parris.

Abigail's mother, Deliverance Hobbs, arrested just three days after her daughter, confirmed that Burroughs was the Devil incarnate, adding that while presiding at the witches' meetings, Burroughs had "pressed them to bewitch all in the village, telling they should do it gradually, not at once, assuring them they should prevail."

Supposedly women flew to the sabbath on the back of monstrous animals. Sometimes the Devil sent a local man to take his place at the gathering. From *Compendium Maleficarum* (Compilation of Witchcraft) by Francesco-Maria Guazzo, 1608. This book was in the Mather Library

Once arrested, everything about Burroughs propelled him to the gallows. A Harvard graduate, he had shown carelessness about the ceremonies of religion, conceding that he had never had his young sons baptized. His home at Casco (present day Portland, Maine), he admitted, was full of toads—from ancient times a symbol of evil. Even his appearance and physique went against him. Black haired and dark complexioned in a community of fair-skinned, blue-eyed Englishmen, he was unusually short. Even so, several witnesses testified to his prodigious strength, one remembering how with just two fingers of one hand Burroughs had lifted a heavy barrel loaded with molasses and carried it several feet.

The cooperation of Abigail and Deliverance Hobbs resulted in their release to freedom. But the Reverend Burroughs was hanged on Friday, August 19. Three other men and the still-defiant Martha Carrier went to the gallows that same day. One was John Proctor, antagonizing the authorities right up to the end, assuring them he could "whip the Devil out of" the shrieking young girls. Another was John Willard of Salem Village, a former constable who had helped to bring the first accused witches to jail, but then turned against the proceedings, only to have the proceeders turn against him.

The fourth man—and fifth member of this defiant, unrepentant group—was seventy-year-old George Jacobs of Salem Town. Master of one of the oldest of the young girls, twenty-year-old Sarah Churchill, this grandfather with the white flowing hair had viewed her and her friends in action and then pronounced them all "witch bitch."

This picture illustrating a seventeenth century English chapbook represents the popular view of old women. —COURTESY BRITISH LIBRARY

CHAPTER FIFTEEN

"The Devil's Kingdom"

No one has ever questioned the right of Wilmot "Mammy" Reed to call herself a witch. Not any of her neighbors in 1692. And not anyone else ever since.*

Hearing of great feats claimed over the years by this seventy-year-old fisherman's wife from the neighboring village of Marblehead, the court had her brought to Salem on May 28. Here and there the court dropped hints that she was expected to help by adding her supernatural powers to the testimony of the afflicted young girls. Stories coming out of Marblehead told how she had caused milk to curdle the moment it came out of the cow or turned newly churned butter into wool.

In the hearing room itself, twenty-nine-year-old Charity Pitman of Marblehead repeated some old gossip, which enhanced Mammy Reed's reputation—and at the same time explained how Salem first heard of her. It seems that a Mrs. Syms of Salem Town had accused Mammy Reed's servant girl, Martha Lawrence, of stealing and threatened to take the girl

---

* Some women chose to practice witchcraft of their own accord; a far larger number had the role or label thrust on them by society. Mammy Reed was one who professed witchcraft, claiming the ability to hex enemies and help friends.

to Judge Hathorne unless she returned the goods. Hearing this, Mammy Reed lashed out at Mrs. Syms with a curse: Mrs. Syms would never again be able to relieve her body of natural wastes. Sure enough, just a short time after, "Mrs. Syms was taken with the distemper of dry belly-ache, and so continued for many months."

But Mammy Reed proved stubbornly uncooperative, refusing to help convict anyone else of witchcraft. To the questions of the judges, she continually retorted: "I know nothing about it." Consequently, this old woman, long considered quaintly harmless at home in Marblehead, made Salem tremble at the prospect of her remaining alive. The court turned on her, changed her status from friendly witness to hostile defendant, and sent her to the gallows on September 22.

As a widely acknowledged, still-active witch, she was the perfect sacrifice. Undoubtedly her hanging would set an example to others similarly inclined, and at the same time satisfy the requirement of scourging Salem, and the whole county of Essex, of evil to make way for the return of the good life.

Another very old woman from a tiny fishing village was arrested at the same time as Mammy Reed. She was seventy-five-year-old Mary Perkins Bradbury of neighboring Salisbury. At her trial, she was forced to listen as various tidbits from the folklore of women and evil were dug up to prove her witchery. Young Richard Carr testified that thirteen years before, after a heated dispute between his family and Mary Bradbury, he and a friend, Zerubabel Endicott, both

> saw Mrs. Bradbury go into her gate, turn the corner, and immediately there darted out of her gate a blue boar and darted at my father's horse's legs, which made him stumble . . . My father said, "Boys, what do you see?" We both answered, "A blue boar."

Immediately following this direct testimony, Stephen Sewall, clerk of the court, added his own incriminating deduction, lest anyone miss the connection:

> They all concluded that it was Mrs. Bradbury that so appeared as a blue boar.

Further besmirching Mrs. Bradbury, thirty-one-year-old Samuel Endicott, brother of Zerubabel, told how Mrs. Bradbury sold two large wooden containers of butter at Boston.

Witches have the power to cause storms. An illustration from the *Compendium Maleficarum* by Francesco-Maria Guazzo, 1608.

Purchaser was the recently deceased Capt. Samuel Smith, about to set out on an ocean mission. After three weeks at sea, crew member Endicott recalled:

> Our men were not able to eat [the butter], it stunk so, and run with maggots, which made the men very much

disturbed about it, and would often say that they heard Mrs. Bradbury was a witch, and that they verily believed she was so, or else she would not have served the captain so as to sell him such butter.

Furthermore, Samuel Endicott said that when a violent storm at sea damaged the ship, the sailors had visions of a woman wearing "a white cap and white neck cloth" and were certain that it was the witch, Mary Bradbury. She was convicted on September 6, 1692, but with the help of devoted friends managed to escape from jail and die a natural death sometime later.

MARY EASTY, one of seven others who went to the gallows the same day as Mammy Reed, makes humans proud of their history.

This fifty-seven-year-old woman, who lived with her husband Isaac and their seven children on one of Topsfield's largest farms, had three serious strikes against her when the witch hunt began. (1) Ann Putnam, Sr., the firebrand mother of Ann, Jr., and actual leader of the young girls, had called Mary Easty a witch who was the daughter of a witch—along with her sisters, Rebecca Towne Nurse, and Sarah Towne Cloyce. (2) Charges had been made to stick against Mary Easty's sister Rebecca who, though the case against her had been weak enough for dismissal, was retried, condemned, and hanged on July 19. (3) Mary Easty's family was deeply involved in the Topsfield land disputes and feuds with the Salem Village faction led by the Putnams.

An obviously intelligent woman who analyzed the problem posed by court procedure, she proposed a specific solution. She petitioned the court to act as counsel for her and her sister Sarah Cloyce, and asked that witnesses friendly to them be permitted to testify. Theoretically, judges were charged with responsibility for helping the accused, as well as hearing the testimony of the accusers and then deciding guilt or innocence. In practice, however, judges concentrated only on finding the defendants guilty, never on proving their innocence. Worse, there were no safeguards for defendants—no lawyers, no cross-examination of witnesses, no caution on the use of gossip or hearsay evidence.

When first arrested on April 21, she defied the judges to prove the charges against her, only to find herself slapped into prison until May 18, when unexpectedly she was released. Almost before she had even tasted the joys of freedom, she was rearrested three days later after being roused from sleep in the middle of the night and snatched from bed as her husband watched helplessly. Recounting the story of her second arrest almost twenty years later, her husband labelled it "a hellish molestation."

Poignantly, eloquently, she addressed the court and the governor, following her sentence of hanging—appealing to their intelligence and humanity, while gently reminding them of their obligations to posterity:

Your poor and humble petitioner knowing my own innocence . . . and seeing plainly the wiles and subtlety of my accusers . . . I petition to your honors not for my own life, for I know I must die and my appointed time is set. But the Lord he knows that if it be possible no more innocent blood may be shed, which undoubtedly cannot be avoided in the way and course you go in. I question not but your honors does to the utmost of your power in the discovery and selecting of witchcraft and witches, and would not be guilty of innocent blood for the world. But by my own innocence I know you are in the wrong way. The Lord in his infinite mercy direct you in this great work. If it be his blessed will that no more innocent blood be shed I would humbly beg of you that your honors would be pleased to examine these afflicted persons strictly and keep them apart some time, and likewise to try some of these confessing witches, I being confident there is several of them has belied themselves and others, as will appear if not in this world, I am sure in the world to come whither I am now going. And I question not but you'll see an alteration of these things they say myself and others having made a league with the Devil we cannot confess. I know and the Lord knows, as will shortly appear, they belie me and so I question not but they do others . . . The Lord knows that . . . I know not the least thing of witchcraft, therefore I cannot, I dare not belie my own soul. I beg your honors not to deny this my humble petition from a poor dying innocent person, and I question not but the Lord will give a blessing to your endeavors.

Mary Easty's fifty-year-old younger sister, Sarah Cloyce, convicted on September 6, just about the time of this petition, was reprieved (following the end of the witch-hunt) and so never went to the gallows.

A third protester who went to the gallows that same September 22 was seventy-year-old Ann Pudeator, a Salem widow. Interestingly, like Mary Easty, she had first been arrested, then released only to be rearrested amid the shrieks and screams of the young girls.

In addition to the usual charges produced at these trials, a piece of frightening folklore used in Europe to put witches to death was resurrected in the case of Goody Pudeator—the use of ointment for evil purposes:

> Goody Pudeator, what did you do with the ointment that you had in the house?

> I never had ointment or oil.

Concocting the witches' ointment. From *De Lamiis* (Concerning Witchcraft) by Ulrich Molitor, 1489.—COURTESY HARVARD THEATRE COLLECTION

But what was in these things the constable speaks of?

It was grease to make soap of.

But why did you put them in so many things when one would have held all?

The record then notes that she "answered not to the purpose, but the constable said ointments were of several sorts" and there is no further questioning on this subject. Before she went to her death, however, Ann Pudeator petitioned the court to recognize that "false evidence and witnesses" had condemned her to die. One of the witnesses against her, she wrote, "has been formerly whipped and likewise is recorded for a liar."

Still another protester was Martha Corey who denounced the proceedings all the way to the gallows on that same Thursday in September. She had been one of the first arrested—following the slave Tituba, the beggar Sarah Good, and the helplessly bedridden Sarah Osborne (who died in jail). Though Sarah Good had been hanged on July 19, at the second execution ordered by the court, for some reason—never recorded—it took six months to hang Martha Corey who had contemptuously laughed in the judges' faces from the very beginning.

THREE ADDITIONAL WOMEN and one man were put to death at the final hanging on September 22. Alice Parker of Salem got into trouble by collecting her drunk husband John at Beadle's, the local tavern, where she publicly scolded him for deserting the family, and used angry words also for the other men present who were pouring the family income into drink. One of these men, forty-year-old Jonathan Westgate, had his revenge, as chief witness at her trial. Ironically, her arrest on May 12 took place before the magistrates in Beadle's tavern.

The widow Mary Parker of Andover—no relation—was arrested very late, on September 1, and went to the gallows just three weeks afterwards on charges so vague and heartless that they are omitted from most accounts. An old woman, she was found lying in the dirt and snow by Jonathan Bullock, described as thirty-six, with no further identification. He and some friends carried her lifeless body to her home and proceeded to remove her clothes before putting her to rest. Suddenly, he recalled, "she rises up and laughs in our faces." He then pronounced her a witch.

Even less is known about Margaret Scott of Rowley. Except for about four sentences repeating the usual routine—by someone named Francis Wyman, himself lost to history—all the records in her case have disappeared or been destroyed.

The one man executed that day was forty-six-year-old Samuel Wardwell of Andover. He had made a confession, which he later took back, that sometimes he told fortunes that came true, and that when any creature came into his field he would "bid the Devil take it." This is the only information available on the case against him.

OLD ANN FOSTER, Andover widow and grandmother, cheated the hangman by wasting to death in jail. At her trial she had testified about flying off with Martha Carrier to a witches' meeting. Her final words, officially recorded, ran wild enough to scare any living man about the powers of women allied with the Devil:

> She heard some of the witches say that there were three hundred and five in the whole county, and that they would ruin that place the Village . . . She further confessed that the discourse among the witches at the meeting at Salem Village was that they would afflict there to set up the Devil's kingdom.

The witch-hunt ended with the last hanging on September 22, 1692. Fourteen women and six men had been put to death. Another eleven women were convicted of witchcraft but never hanged. Five of this group were lucky enough to survive to a period of relative calm, when they were reprieved. Two had their execution postponed for pregnancy, and were later released. One escaped with the help of friends. Another, the slave Tituba, was kept in jail till she was sold to pay her jail costs. Sarah Osborne and Ann Foster who died in jail should by all rights be added to the list of the twenty executed for witchcraft.

Of the six men put to death, three are quoted as lashing out at the witch-hunt. The deaths of the other three men convicted of witchcraft defy neat categorization.

A REMARK QUOTED by twenty-seven-year-old Daniel Elliott, a friendly witness testifying to save the life of Elizabeth Proctor, has been quoted over and over again to explain the Salem outbreak. He reported that one of the young girls, challenged for crying out, "There's [the specter of] Goody Proctor," took it all back, conceding that "She did it for sport. They must have some sport."

The girls made the most noise at the trials and so have attracted most of the attention ever since. Following their instant success against Sarah Good and Sarah Osborne, they were pressed into service, repeating their routine of hallucinations and fits. In reality, however, the enemies of those accused of witchcraft were merely hiding behind the girls' rantings and ravings, allowing them to set the tone for all examinations. Thus, most of the witnesses were male, sixty-three out of eighty-four testifying. Also, men who were both adult and powerful played the decisive roles in the prosecution. These were the judges, the village minister Samuel Parris and his staunch allies Nathaniel and John Putnam, and the intellectual inquisitor Cotton Mather.

Too frequently, Salem is treated in a vacuum, without reference to centuries of European history or folklore. In this connection, Daniel Elliott's report about one of the young girls is illuminated by a story long told in Europe—and finally recorded by the Brothers Grimm in the nineteenth century. The tale, "Frau Trude," demonstrates the universality of childish rebellion against adult authority:

There was once a young girl who was stubborn and mean and tired of everything in her life. Whenever her parents asked her to do anything, she would say, "Do it yourself!" She never considered the feelings of others, only what she wanted. So one day she told her parents, "I'm going to Frau Trude's house in the woods, I've heard that she does all kinds of strange things and her house is really a sight to see." But her parents answered, "Frau Trude is evil, a dangerous woman. If you go to her, we will never allow you in our house again."

Nonetheless, the girl's curiosity got the better of her and she sought the house of Frau Trude. But when Frau Trude answered the door, she saw a terrified girl on her steps. "What's wrong, my child?" asked Frau Trude. "Oh!" cried the girl, "I saw a black man standing at your door!"

"That was a collier," explained Frau Trude.

"Next I saw a green man," trembled the girl.

"That was a hunter," said Frau Trude.

"Then I saw a red man."

"That was a butcher."

"But then, oh, then, I looked into the window of your house and instead of you it was the Devil I saw with his head all in flames."

"Aha, at last you have beheld the witch as she really is. I have awaited your arrival many years. Finally, there will be some light to see by." And with these words Frau Trude turned the girl into a wooden log, which she tossed onto the fire, and there she sat, warming herself by the flames.

(Adapted from Grimm, #43)

EVERY IMAGINABLE THESIS has been used to explain the outbreak in Salem: hysteria of bored young girls relishing the special attention paid to their every word and gesture by the entire community; disputes over property; the haves versus the have-nots; ergot—rye mold—which contaminated the bread eaten and led to strange behavior; the influence of "Indian paganism."

And so on. And so forth.

Theories come and go, but the statistics remain the same: Fourteen of twenty put to death as witches at Salem in 1692 were women. Twenty-five of thirty-one convicted of witchcraft were women. One hundred four of one hundred forty-one accused witches were women.

FOR ALL PRACTICAL PURPOSES the Great Witch Hunt petered out at Salem in 1692, laid to rest by the onset of the scientific revolution and the Age of Reason. But not before it had subordinated women to men with a vengeance—and with effects still felt today. Overwhelmingly, power continues to be in the hands of men.

"Linda Maestra" (Attractive Teacher). Etching by Francisco
Goya. *Capricho 68.*—COURTESY FOGG MUSEUM OF ART,
HARVARD UNIVERSITY

Aftermath

S ome one hundred years after the end of the Great Witch Hunt, Spain's great artist Francisco Goya (1746–1828) caricatured witchcraft, carefully including all the details that had once frightened and fascinated society. In the etching titled "Linda Maestra" (Attractive Teacher), a witch that is old, a hag, and a woman is passing on her secrets to the young, female apprentice. They fly through the air on a broomstick, symbolic of a male demon (the legendary *incubus*, or nightmare). Overhead hovers the owl, the visible guise of Adam's first wife Lilith.

To the question of whether such superstitions and folklore involving the practice of evil had been more easily applied to women than to men, the observable, historical answer is yes.

To the question of whether the long Witch Hunt was a conspiracy of men against women, the answer is no.

But this negative response has to be qualified. There was not the slightest need for a conspiracy. Female evil and male innocence were accepted as unquestioningly as the appearance of the moon every night and the sun every day. From birth even the humblest male, if he lived, was ordained to be a member of the superior human species, and woman subordinate to him.

Add to all this the need to find those responsible when crisis and cataclysm occurred. Woman, the conspicuous incarnation of evil, was the obvious scapegoat—especially if she attracted attention by rebelling against the established order, or by disturbing the natural setup in any way—or if she was past her ability to bear children, her sole contribution to society and the only justification for allowing her to share man's hard-won food, clothing, and shelter in the first place.

NO LONGER ARE WOMEN BURNED or hanged as witches, or synonymous with evil. Still, Eugene McCarthy, third party candidate in the Presidential election of 1976, exploded in words that would have aroused the immediate sympathy of any medieval man. Miffed at receiving only one percent of the popular vote nationally, former Senator McCarthy was quoted by United Press International, November 5, 1976:

> We have created a new era of politics where the great mother goddess is the president of the League of Women Voters and the minor gods are the three presidents of the television networks. They're the ones who decide who the candidates are and no one else has a chance.

Even in print, the speaker's bitter sarcasm emerges with "great" placed before "goddess" and "minor" before "gods." Imagine then the original strength of identical sentiments during the Great Witch Hunt.

Whatever Senator McCarthy may think, however, women continue to be excluded from power. Figures from 1977 and 1991 reveal only marginal change. In 1977, in the United States, two of fifty governors were women; in 1991, two of fifty governors are women. In 1977, eighteen of four hundred thirty-five voting members (4.1 percent) of the House of Representatives were female; in 1991, the number has increased to twenty-nine (6.6 percent in a female population of fifty-plus percent). In 1977, among one hundred senators, not one was a woman; in 1991, there are two women (2 percent) in the Senate. For the first time in U.S. history, one out of the nine justices on the Supreme Court is a woman, and in 1984, also for the first time, one of the two major political parties nominated a woman, though her ticket did not win the election, meaning that no woman has ever served as President or Vice President of the U.S.

WOMAN'S SPECIAL SKILLS and instincts are desperately needed in a world still plagued by war and by careless ravaging of the earth. The solution for using the talents of women and men equally must somehow be lying in the lap of the goddesses. Certainly, the record of the gods has not been impressive.

A Note on Spelling, Dates, Superb Libraries, and Perceptive Critics

Europe adopted the Gregorian calendar in 1582, and Great Britain and her colonies in 1752. For all practical purposes, however, *Riding the Nightmare* abandons Europe before the changeover, and remains in the British Empire till 1692. Therefore, no attempt has been made to add ten days to dates as originally recorded under the Old Julian calendar, in order to make them conform with the modern, or Gregorian, calendar. The one exception here is that January, February, and most of March, considered the last months of the year under the old Julian calendar, are written in the book as the first, second, and third months, as in modern calendars. For example, it seems both pointless and needlessly confusing to list the arrest date of Sarah Good, Sarah Osborne, and Tituba as February 29, 1691, or even as February 29, 1691/2. The date is given simply as February 29, 1692.

Nevertheless, spelling and punctuation have been modernized, whenever necessary, for easier understanding. There is no danger of distorting the flavor of the original, since copies of the same document often turn up with completely different spelling and punctuation. Grammar has been left alone, except when utterly incomprehensible.

The book would have been impossible without the unmatched research facilities of the Boston area. Special gratitude is due to Cary Memorial Library, Lexington, where the reference staff is constantly adding new publications to its already impressive colonial history resources. The Library of Essex Institute, Salem, and Reference Librarian Mrs. Arthur R. Norton supplied a constant stream of source material unavailable anywhere else. Also most helpful were the resources and personnel of the Department of Rare Books and Manuscripts, as well as the Research and Social Sciences Departments, of the Boston Public Library; and the collection of rare books and manuscripts at Houghton Library, Harvard.

It was a great privilege to interview Charles S. Tapley, descendant of Rebecca Nurse and author of *Rebecca Nurse, Saint but Witch Victim.*

Editor Jean Karl of Atheneum tamed the original unwieldy manuscript and provided an indispensable sense of direction.

Natalie Miller, equal opportunity specialist for the Massachusetts Department of Education, borrowed hours from her precious spare time to read and comment perceptively on the entire manuscript. Burton L. Williams, sympathetic critic, and Wendy D. Williams, resident feminist, have given helpful advice and support whenever needed. And Ailene S. Goodman made time in an inhumanly busy schedule to track down two paintings in Vienna.

Bibliography

Some sources listed below bear dates of the late eighteenth, nineteenth, or twentieth centuries, although they were contemporary with, or sometimes even preceded, the Great Witch Hunt. There are several reasons: (1) publication occurred after the author's death, or (2) official records were found or transcribed long after the event, or (3) to their everlasting glory, publishers have reprinted certain rare old books, making them accessible in general libraries.

Primary Sources

I. Bibles

Bishops' Bible of 1568. London: Richard Jugg, 1572.

Cranmer Bible (called also The Great Bible of 1539).

Cranmer Bible. London: Edward Whitchurche, printer, 1549.

Guttenberg Bible. Mainz, Germany, 1456.

The Holy Bible, Revised Standard Version. New York: The World Publishing Company, 1962.

King James' Bible, 1611.

Luther's Bible. Wittenberg, Germany: 1551.

Matthew's Bible. London: John Daye and William Seres, 1537.

La Saincte Bible. Lyon, France: Sebastian Honorate, 1566.

II. European History and Philosophy

AQUINAS, ST. THOMAS. *The Summa Theologica.* Translated by Fathers of the English Dominican Province. Part I. New York: Benziger Brothers, 1912 and 1947.

ARISTOTLE. *Generation of Animals*. Translated by A. L. Peck. Cambridge, Mass.: Harvard University Press, 1943.

———. *Politics and Poetics*. Translated by B. Jowett and T. Twining. New York: Viking Press, Compass Books Edition, 1957.

AUGUSTINE, ST. *The City of God Against the Pagans*. Cambridge, Mass.: Harvard University Press, 1965–1966.

BODIN, JEAN. *The Six Bookes of a Commonweale*. Translated by Richard Knolles. London: G. Bishop, 1606.

CALVIN, JOHN. *The Institution of Christian Religion*. Translated by Thomas Norton. London: Henrie Middleton, 1582.

COOKE, ALEXANDER. *Pope Joane: A Dialogue betweene a Protestant and a Papist, Manifestly proving that a woman called Joane was Pope of Rome, against the surmises and objections made to the contrarie*. London: E. Blunt and W. Barret, 1610.

GREGORY, BISHOP OF TOURS. *History of the Franks*. Edited by Ernest Brenaut. New York: Octagon Books, Inc., 1965.

HEYWOOD, THOMAS /T. H. GENT/. *The Generall Historie of Women of the most holy, and prophane: the most Famous and Infamous in all Ages*. London: W. H., 1657.

HOBBES, THOMAS. *Leviathan*. New York: E. P. Dutton & Co. Inc., 1943.

LUTHER, MARTIN. *Table Talk*. Edited and translated by William Hazlitt. London: George Bell & Sons, 1883.

PALMER, PAUL F., S.J., S.T.D., ed. *Mary in the Documents of the Church*. Westminster, Maryland: The Newman Press, 1952.

PITCAIRN, ROBERT. *Criminal Trials in Scotland from A.D. 1488 to A.D. 1624 . . . Compiled from the Original Records and MSS*. 4 vols. Edinburgh: William Tait, 1833.

SHARP, JANE. *The Midwives Book or the whole Art of Midwifery. . . .* London: Printed for Simon Miller, at the Star at the West End of St. Paul's, 1671.

(Jane Sharp shows profound knowledge of male and female anatomy, the Bible, and mythology. The first eighty pages are devoted to "an anatomical description of the parts of men and women." Part II, 81–162. "What is requisite for procreation, signs of a woman's being with child . . . and how the child is formed in the womb.")

TAPPERT, THEODORE G., ed. *Table Talk.* Luther's Works, vol. 54. Philadelphia: Fortress Press, 1967.

III. *Mythology, Folklore, and Literature*

APOLLONIUS OF RHODES. *The Voyage of Argo.* Translated by E. V. Rieu. England: Penguin Books, 1959.

APULEIUS. *The Golden Ass.* Translated by Jack Lindsay. Bloomington, Indiana: Indiana University Press, 1960.

BARING-GOULD, WILLIAM S. & CEIL. *The Annotated Mother Goose.* New York: Clarkson N. Potter, Inc., 1962.

BOCCACCIO, GIOVANNI. *The Decameron.* Garden City, N.Y.: Garden City Books, 1930.

BUNYAN, JOHN. *Grace Abounding to the Chief of Sinners and The Pilgrim's Progress.* New York: Oxford University Press, 1966.

CHAUCER, GEOFFREY. *The Canterbury Tales.* Translated by Nevill Coghill. Baltimore, Maryland: Penguin Books, 1967.

Epstein, Rabbi Dr. I., ed. The Babylonian Talmud. London: The Soncino Press, 1935.

EURIPIDES. *Medea and Other Plays.* Translated by Philip Vellacott. Baltimore: Penguin Books Inc., 1963.

GINZBERG, LOUIS. *The Legends of the Jews.* 7 vols. Philadelphia: The Jewish Publication Society of America, 1912.

GRIMM, JACOB AND WILHELM. *The Complete Grimm's Fairy Tales.* New York: Pantheon Books, 1944.

HERODOTUS. *Complete Works.* Translated by A. D. Godley. Cambridge, Mass.: Harvard University Press, 1921.
(Contains many legends of the Amazons.)

HOMER. *The Odyssey.* Translated by Robert Fitzgerald. Garden City, New York: Anchor Books, Doubleday & Company, Inc.
———. *The Homeric Hymns.* Translated by Daryl Hine. New York: Atheneum, 1972.

HUSSEY, MAURICE, trans. into modern English. *The Chester Mystery Plays.* London: Heinemann, 1957.

KING, L. W., ED. *The Seven Tablets of Creation.* London: Luzac and Co., 1902.

(Babylonian creation myth which describes the downfall of the mother goddess, Tiamat.)

LELAND, CHARLES GODFREY AND PRINCE, JOHN DYNELEY, trans. *Kuloskap the Master and other Algonkin Poems.* New York: Funk and Wagnalls, 1902.

OVID. *The Art of Love and Other Poems.* Translated by J. H. Mozley. Cambridge, Mass.: Harvard University Press, 1929.

————. *The Metamorphoses.* Translated by Horace Gregory. New York: The Viking Press, Inc., 1958.

PLUTARCH. *Moralia.* Vol. 5. Translated by Frank Cole Babbitt. Cambridge, Mass.: Harvard University Press, 1936.

SCHOLEM, GERSHOM G., ED. *Zohar, The Book of Splendor.* New York: Schocken Books, 1949.

SPENSER, EDMUND. *The Faerie Queene in Complete Works.* Edited by R. Morris. London: Macmillan, 1895.

SPERLING, HARRY AND SIMON, MAURICE, trans. *The Zohar.* London: The Soncino Press, 1949.

(Contains many passages on Lilith and witchcraft.)

STONE, BRIAN, trans. *Medieval English Verse.* Baltimore, Maryland: Penguin Books, Inc., 1964.

STRABO. *The Geography of Strabo.* Translated by Horace Leonard Jones. Cambridge, Mass.: Harvard University Press, 1928.

VORAGINE, JACOBO. *The Golden Legend or Lives of the Saints.* Translated by William Caxton. 7 vols. London: J. M. Dent and Co., 1900.

IV. New England

BURR, GEORGE LINCOLN, ED. *Narratives of the Witchcraft Cases, 1648–1706.* New York: Barnes & Noble, 1914, 1946, 1972.

COTTON, JOHN. *Spiritual Milk for Babes Drawn out of the Breasts of both Testaments. . . .* London: Printed for Peter Parker, near Cree-Church, 1668.

FROST, ARCHIE N. (clerk of courts). *Salem Witchcraft-1692.*

3 vols. 1938. (Verbatim transcriptions of Salem witchcraft papers.)

HUTCHINSON, THOMAS. *The History of the Colony and Province of Massachusetts Bay.* Edited by Lawrence Mayo. 3 vols. Cambridge, Mass.: Harvard University Press, 1936. (See especially "The Examination of Mrs. Ann Hutchinson at the Court of Newton," vol. 2, appendix 2, pp. 336–391.)

JOHNSON, EDWARD. *Wonder Working Providence of Sion's Savior in New England, 1651.* Edited by J. Franklin Jameson. New York: Barnes & Noble, 1959.

JOSSELYN, JOHN. *An Account of Two Voyages to New-England, Made during the years 1638, 1663.* Boston: William Veazie, 1865.

————. *New-England's Rarities.* London: G. Widdowes at the Green Dragon in St. Paul's Church yard, 1672, Boston: William Veazie, 1865.

MATHER, COTTON. *Diary, 1681–1709.* Edited by Worthington Chauncey Ford. Vol. 1. 1911. Reprint. New York: Frederick Ungar, n.d.

————. *Magnalia Christi Americana or The Ecclesiastical History of New England from Its First Planting, in the Year 1620, unto the year of our Lord 1698.* 2 vols. Hartford: Silas Andrus & Son, 1702, 1853.

————. *Selections from Cotton Mather.* Edited by Kenneth B. Murdock. New York: Hafner Publishing Co., 1965.

MAULE, THOMAS. *Truth held forth and maintained.* Noah Clap: 1695.

MORTON, THOMAS. *New English Canaan.* 3 vols. Vol. 1 "setting forth the original of the Natives, their Manners and Customs . . ."; vol. 2 "setting forth the natural endowments of the country . . ."; vol. 3 "setting forth what people are planted there . . ." Amsterdam: Jacob Frederick Stam, 1637.

PARRIS, REV. SAMUEL. "Sermons." From original MS in Conn. Historical Society's collection.

PHILATHES, THO. *New-England Persecutors Mauled With their own Weapons.* Printed about 1697.

ROWLANDSON, MARY. *The Narrative of the Captivity and Resto-*

ration of Mrs. Mary Rowlandson. Boston: Houghton-Mifflin, 1930. (May also be found in *Narratives of the Indian Wars, 1675–1699.* Edited by Charles H. Lincoln. New York: Barnes & Noble, 1959, pp. 112–167 and in *The Colonial Image.* Edited by John C. Miller. New York: George Braziller, 1962.

WILLIAM STOUGHTON MS AM. 48 (Sentencing of Rebecca Nurse et al). Boston: Boston Public Library.

TULLEY, JOHN. *An Almanack For the Year of our Lord, 1691, 1692.* Cambridge, Mass.: Samuel Green, & Bartholomew Green, 1691, 1692.

———. *An Almanack For the Year of our Lord, 1693.* Boston: Benjamin Harris for Samuel Phillips, 1693.

WINTHROP, JOHN. *History of New England, 1630–1649.* Edited by James Kendall Hosmer. 2 vols. New York: Barnes & Noble, 1959. (Included is a section from "A Short Story of the Rise, Reign, and Ruin of the Antinomians" in which Winthrop discusses Anne Hutchinson.)

———. *The History of New England from 1630 to 1649.* Vol. 1. Edited by James Savage. Boston: Phelps and Farnham, 1825. (Preferable to Hosmer's editing of the Winthrop journal because Savage makes no attempt to turn the Puritans into the Victorian model of modesty and chastity. However, Hosmer, recently republished, is more readily obtainable.)

WOOD, WILLIAM. *New England's Prospect.* London: John Bellamie, 1634.

V. Witchcraft Tracts and Chapbooks

BAXTER, RICHARD. *The Certainty of the World of Spirits Fully Evinced,* 1691. Reprint London: Joseph Smith, 1693; High Holborn, 1834.

BEIGEL, DR. HERMAN. *The Examination and Confession of Certain Witches at Chelmsford in the County of Essex, 1565.* London: 1864.

BERNARD, RICHARD. *A Guide to Grand Jury Men.* London: Felix Kingston for Ed. Blackmore, 1627.

BLACK, GEORGE F., ED. *Witchcraft in Scotland 1510–1727*. New York: Arno Press Inc., 1938, 1971.

BODIN, JEAN. *De Magorum Daemonomania*. Basil: 1581.

BOGUET, HENRY. *An Examen of Witches*. Lyons: 1590. Reprint. Great Britain: John Rodker, 1929, 1971.

CASAUBON, MERIC. *Of Credulity and Incredulity in things Natural, Civil and Divine*. London: T. Garthwait, 1668.

COTTA, JOHN. *The Infallible True and Assured Witch: Or, The Second Edition of the Tryall of Witch-craft Shewing the Right and True Methode of the Discoverie*. London: 1624.

FILMER, SIR ROBERT. *An Advertisement to the Jury-Men of England Touching Witches*. London: 1653.

GAULE, JOHN. *Select Cases of Conscience Touching Witches and Witchcraft*. London: W. Wilson, 1646.

GLANVIL, JOSEPH. *Saducismus Triumphatus or, Full and Plain Evidence concerning Witches and Apparitions*. London: J. Collin, 1681.

GRAINGE, WILLIAM. Introduction and Notes to *Fairfax Daemonologia*, by Edward Fairfax. 1882. Reprint. New York: Barnes & Noble Inc., 1971.

HALE, JOHN. *A Modest Inquiry into the Nature of Witchcraft*. 1702. Reprint. Bainbridge, New York: York Mail-Print, Inc. 1973. Introduction by Richard Trask, Archivist, Danvers, Mass.

HUTCHINSON, FRANCIS. *Historical Essay Concerning Witchcraft*. London: R. Knaplock and D. Midwinter, 1718.

JAMES I, KING OF ENGLAND. *Daemonologie,* 1597. Reprint. London: Curwen Press, 1924.

KRAMER, HEINRICH AND SPRENGER, JAMES. *The Malleus Maleficarum*. 1486. Reprint. New York: Dover Publications, Inc., 1971.

DE LOIER, PETER. *A treatise of specters*. . . . London: Mathew Lownes, 1605.
(This book is an excellent bridge between mythology and witchcraft belief.)

MATHER, COTTON. *The Wonders of the Invisible World*. . . . Boston: 1693.

PERKINS, M. WILLIAM. *A Discourse of the Damned Art of Witchcraft.* . . . Cambridge, England: University of Cambridge, Thomas Pickering, 1618.

POTTS, THOMAS. *The Trial of the Lancaster Witches.* 1613. Edited by G. B. Harrison. London: Peter Davies, 1929. Reprint. New York: Barnes & Noble Inc., 1971.

R. D. *The Strange and Prodigious Religions, Customs, and Manners, of Sundry Nations.* London: Hen. Rhodes, 1688.

SCOT, REGINALD. *The Discoverie of Witchcraft.* 1584. Reprint. New York: Dover Publications, Inc., 1972.

WAGSTAFFE, JOHN. *The Question of Witchcraft Debated.* London: Edw. Millington, 1671.

WEBSTER, JOHN. *The Displaying of Supposed Witchcraft,* et. London: Jonas Moore, 1677.

WOODWARD, W. ELLIOT, ED. *Records of Salem Witchcraft, Copied from the Original Documents.* New York: Da Capo Press, 1969.

(Not as complete as the W.P.A. typescript at Essex Institute, Salem, Mass., but more widely available.)

Secondary Sources

I. Periodicals

DEMOS, JOHN. "Underlying Themes of Witchcraft in Salem." *American Historical Review* (June, 1970).

FOWLER, SAMUEL P. "Samuel Parris." *Essex Institute Proceedings* 2 (1856): 48–69.

KOCH, DONALD WARNER. "Income Distribution and Political Structure in Seventeenth-Century Salem, Massachusetts." *Essex Institute Collections* 105 (1969): 50–69.

PHILLIPS, HENRY JR. "Old-Time Superstitions." Reprint from *The Penn. Monthly* (1882). (at Salem's Essex Institute.)

SIPLE, ELLA S. "Some Recently Identified Tapestries in the Gardner Museum in Boston." *The Burlington Magazine,* November, 1930, pp. 236–241.

TRIBLE, PHYLLIS. "Depatriarchalizing in Biblical Tradition." *Journal of American Academy of Religion*, 41 (March, 1973): 30–48.

II. *Reference*

EAST, WILLIAM G. *The Geography behind History*. London: T. Nelson and Sons, Ltd., 1939.

GRAVES, ROBERT. *New Larousse Encyclopedia of Mythology*. Translated by Richard Aldington and Delano Ames. New York: The Hamlyn Publishing Group Limited, 1959.

JOBES, GERTRUDE. *Dictionary of Mythology, Folklore, and Symbols*. New York: The Scarecrow Press, Inc., 1962.

LANGDON, STEPHEN HERBERT. *The Mythology of All Races: Semitic,* edited by John Arnott MacCulloch, vol. 5. Boston: Marshall Jones Company, 1931.

LEACH, MARIA, ED. *Standard Dictionary of Folklore, Mythology, and Legend*. New York: Funk and Wagnalls, 1950.

MULLER, W. MAX. *The Mythology of All Races: Egyptian,* edited by Louis Herbert Gray, vol. 12. Boston: Marshall Jones Company, 1918.

ROBBINS, ROSSELL HOPE. *The Encyclopedia of Witchcraft and Demonology*. New York: Crown Publishers, Inc., 1974.

SCHOLEM, GERSHOM. *Encyclopaedia Judaica*. "Lilith."

———. *Encyclopaedia Judaica*. "Demonology."

III. *Witchcraft*

BAROJA, JULIO CARO. *The World of the Witches*. Chicago: The University of Chicago Press, 1973.

BOYER, PAUL AND NISSENBAUM, STEPHEN. *Salem Possessed: The Social Origins of Witchcraft*. Cambridge, Mass.: Harvard University Press, 1974.

———, eds. *Salem-Village Witchcraft*. Belmont, Calif.: Wadsworth Publishing Co., Inc., 1972.

BRIGGS, K. M. *Pale Hecate's Team*. London: Routledge and Kegan Paul, 1962.

COHN, NORMAN. *Europe's Inner Demons.* London: Chatto & Heinemann for Sussex University Press, 1975.

DOUGLAS, MARY, ED. *Witchcraft Confessions & Accusations.* New York: Tavistock Publications, 1970.

EWEN, C. L'ESTRANGE, ED. *Witch Hunting and Witch Trials.* London: Kegan Paul, Trench, Trubner & Co., Ltd., 1929.

FELT, JOSEPH B. *Annals of Salem.* Vol. 2, 2nd edition. Salem and Boston: W. & S. D. Ives, James Munroe & Co., 1849.

FORBES, THOMAS ROGERS. *The Midwife and the Witch.* New Haven: Yale University Press, 1966.

HANSEN, CHADWICK. *Witchcraft at Salem.* New York: George Braziller, 1969.

Kieckhefer, Richard. *European Witch Trials.* Berkeley, Calif.: University of California Press, 1976.

KITTREDGE, GEORGE LYMAN. *Witchcraft in Old and New England.* New York: Atheneum, 1972.

LEA, HENRY CHARLES. *Materials Toward A History of Witchcraft.* Edited by Arthur C. Howland. 3 vols. New York: Thomas Yoseloff, 1957.

MACFARLANE, A. D. J. *Witchcraft in Tudor and Stuart England.* New York: Harper & Row, Publishers, Inc., 1970.

MICHELET, JULES. *Satanism and Witchcraft.* Secaucus, N.J.: Lyle Stuart, 1939, 1862.

MIDELFORT, H. D. ERIK. *Witch Hunting in Southwestern Germany, 1562–1684.* Stanford, Calif.: Stanford University Press, 1972.

MONTER, E. WILLIAM, ED. *European Witchcraft.* New York: John Wiley & Sons, Inc., 1969.

———. *Witchcraft in France and Switzerland.* Ithaca, N.Y.: Cornell University Press, 1976.

NEVINS, WINFIELD S. *Witchcraft in Salem Village in 1692.* New York: Burt Franklin, 1916, 1971.

NOTESTEIN, WALLACE. *A History of Witchcraft in England From 1588 to 1718.* New York: Thomas Y. Crowell Company, 1968.

PARRINDER, GEOFFREY. *Witchcraft: European and African.* London: Faber and Faber, 1970.

PERLEY, SIDNEY. *The History of Salem, Massachusetts,* Vol. 3, 1671–1716. Salem, Mass.: Sidney Perley, 1928. (See esp. Ch. 14, "The Witchcraft Delusion, 254–295.)

PHILLIPS, JAMES DUNCAN. *Salem in the Seventeenth Century.* Boston: Houghton Mifflin, 1933.

RUSSELL, JEFFREY BURTON. *Witchcraft in the Middle Ages.* Ithaca, N.Y.: Cornell University Press, 1972.

SEGUIN, ROBERT-LIONEL. *La Sorcellerie au Canada Français du XVIIe au XIXe Siècles.* Montréal: Ducharme, 1961.

(The only available book on Canadian witchcraft, only minimally helpful here.)

STARKEY, MARION L. *The Devil in Massachusetts.* Garden City, New York: Doubleday & Company, Inc., 1949, 1969.

TAPLEY, CHARLES SUTHERLAND. *Rebecca Nurse, Saint but Witch Victim.* Boston: Marshall Jones, 1930.

THOMAS, KEITH. *Religion and the Decline of Magic.* Great Britain: Penguin Books, 1973.

TINDALL, GILLIAN. *A Handbook on Witches.* New York: Atheneum, 1969.

TREVOR-ROPER, H. R. *The European Witch-Craze.* New York: Harper & Row, Publishers, 1969.

UPHAM, CAROLINE E. *Salem Witchcraft in Outline.* Salem, Mass., The Salem Press, 1891.

(Interesting as an early attempt by a woman to view witchcraft persecution with sympathy for the women involved.)

UPHAM, CHARLES W. *Salem Witchcraft.* 2 vols. New York: Frederick Ungar Publishing Co., 1959.

IV. *Women in Mythology, Religion, and History*

ADDISON, JULIA DE WOLF. *Classic Myths in Art.* Boston: L. C. Page & Company, 1904.

ARMSTRONG, EDWARD A. *The Folklore of Birds.* Boston: Houghton Mifflin, 1959.

BACHOFEN, J. J. *Myth, Religion, and Mother Right.* Translated by Ralph Manheim. Princeton, New Jersey: Bollingen Series 84, 1967.

BAINTON, ROLAND H. *Women of the Reformation in France and England.* 1894. Reprint. Boston: Beacon Press, 1975.

———. *Women of the Reformation in Germany and Italy.* 1894. Reprint. Boston: Beacon Press, 1974.

BARING-GOULD, SABINE. *Curious Myths of the Middle Ages.* 1866–1868. Reprint. New York: University Books, 1967.

BATTIS, EMERY. *Saints and Sectaries: Anne Hutchinson and the Antinomian Controversy in the Massachusetts Bay Colony.* Chapel Hill: University of North Carolina Press, 1962. (Well-researched history but conspicuously unsympathetic to Anne Hutchinson.)

BEARD, MARY R. *Woman as Force in History.* New York: Collier Books, 1946, 1971.

BELL, SUSAN G., ED. *Women: From the Greeks to the French Revolution.* Belmont, Calif.: Wadsworth Publishing Company, Inc., 1973.

BRIFFAULT, ROBERT. *The Mothers.* Abridged by Gordon Rattray Taylor. London: George Allen and Unwin Ltd., 1927, 1959.

CAMPBELL, JOSEPH. *The Masks of God: Occidental Mythology.* New York: The Viking Press, 1964.

CLASEN, CLAUS-PETER. *Anabaptism: A Social History, 1525–1618 in Switzerland, Austria, Moravia, South and Central Germany.* Ithaca, N.Y.: Cornell University Press, 1972.

COULTON, G. G. *Life in the Middle Ages.* 4 vols. Cambridge, England: Cambridge University Press, 1967.

———. *Medieval Panorama: The English Scene from Conquest to Reformation.* New York: MacMillan, 1947.

DALY, MARY. *Beyond God the Father.* Boston: Beacon Press, 1973.

DAVIDSON, H. R. ELLIS. *Gods and Myths of Northern Europe.* England: Penguin Books Ltd., 1964.

DINER, HELEN. *Mothers and Amazons.* New York: Anchor Press/Doubleday, 1973.

DOUGLAS, MARY. *Natural Symbols: Explorations in Cosmology.* New York: Pantheon Books, 1970.

ELIADE, MIRCEA. *The Sacred and the Profane.* New York: Harcourt, Brace & World, Inc., 1959.

FRAZER, JAMES. *The Golden Bough.* 13 vols. London: MacMillan and Co., Limited, 1913.

GIMPEL, JEAN. *The Medieval Machine: The Industrial Revolution of the Middle Ages.* New York: Holt, Rinehart and Winston, 1976.

HARDING, M. ESTHER. *Woman's Mysteries.* New York: Bantam Books, 1971.

HEER, FRIEDRICH. *The Medieval World, Europe, 1100–1350.* Translated by Janet Sondheimer. New York: Mentor, 1961.

HILLERBRAND, HANS J. *The World of the Reformation.* New York: Charles Scribner's Sons, 1973.
   (See especially pp. 193–198, "The Reformation and Women.")

JAMESON, MRS. *Sacred and Legendary Art.* Vol. 2. 1896. Reprint. New York: AMS Press, 1970.

LEHMANN, ANDRÉÉ. *Le Role de la Femme au Moyen Age.* Paris: Editions Berger-Levrault, 1952.

LEIGHTON, ANN. *Early American Gardens.* Boston: Houghton Mifflin Company, 1970.
   (For superstitions associated with herbs and plants.)

LERNER, ROBERT E. *The Heresy of the Free Spirit in the Later Middle Ages.* Berkeley, Calif.: University of California Press, 1972.

McDONNELL, ERNEST W. *The Beguines and Beghards in Medieval Culture.* New Brunswick, N.J.: Rutgers University Press, 1954.

MILLER, PERRY. *The New England Mind, From Colony to Province.* Cambridge: Harvard University Press, 1953.

—— and Johnson, Thomas H., eds. *The Puritans.* 2 vols. New York: Harper & Row, 1938, 1963.

MOREWEDGE, ROSEMARIE THEE, ED. *The Role of Woman in the Middle Ages.* Albany, N.Y.: State University of New York Press, 1975.
   (See especially "Life Expectancies for Women in Medieval Society," by David Herlihy, pp. 1–22.)

NEUMANN, ERICH. *The Great Mother.* Translated by Ralph Manheim. Bollingen Series 47. Princeton, N.J.: Princeton University Press, 1955.

————. *The Origins and History of Consciousness.* Translated by R. F. C. Hull. Bollingen Series 42. Princeton, N.J.: Princeton University Press, 1954.

NIGG, WALTER. *The Heretics.* Edited and translated by Richard and Clara Winston. New York: Alfred A. Knopf, 1962.

NORTON, ARTHUR O. *Harvard Text-Books and Reference Books of the Seventeenth Century.* Vol. 27. Massachusetts: Publications of Colonial Society of Massachusetts, 1936.

PATAI, RAPHAEL. *The Hebrew Goddess.* Ktav Publishing House, Inc., 1967.

PERNOUD, RÉGINE. *Joan of Arc by Herself and Her Witnesses.* Translated by Edward Hyams. New York: Stein and Day, 1966.

POMEROY, SARAH B. *Goddesses, Whores, Wives, and Slaves: Women in Classical Antiquity.* New York: Schocken Books, 1975.

POWER, EILEEN. *Medieval People.* New York: Barnes & Noble, 1924, 1963.

————. *Medieval Women.* Edited by M. M. Postan. Cambridge, England: Cambridge University Press, 1975.

REUTHER, ROSEMARY RADFORD, ED. *Religion and Sexism.* New York: Simon and Schuster, 1974.

DE RIENCOURT, AMAURY. *Sex and Power in History.* New York: David McKay Company, Inc., 1974.
(Generally well-researched history but conspicuously unsympathetic to women.)

ROGERS, KATHARINE M. *The Troublesome Helpmate: A History of Misogyny in Literature.* Seattle, Washington: University of Washington Press, 1966.

RUGG, WINNIFRED KING. *Unafraid: A Life of Anne Hutchinson.* Boston: Houghton Mifflin, 1930.

SCHOLEM, GERSHOM. *On the Kabbalah and Its Symbolism.* Translated by Ralph Manheim. New York: Schocken Books, 1965.

SOUTHERN, R. W. *Western Society and the Church in the Middle Ages.* Great Britain: Penguin Books, 1970, 1973.

STENTON, DORIS MARY. *The English Woman in History.* London: George Allen & Unwin Ltd., 1957.

STRAYER, JOSEPH. *The Albigensian Crusades.* New York: Dial Press, 1971.

STUARD, SUSAN MOSHER, ED. *Women in Medieval Society.* Philadelphia, Pa.: University of Pennsylvania Press, 1976.

TAYLOR, G. RATTRAY. *Sex in History.* New York: Vanguard Press, 1955.

THISELTON-DYER, T. F. *Folk-Lore of Women.* London: Elliot Stock, 1906.

TRACHTENBERG, JOSHUA. *Jewish Magic and Superstition.* New York: Atheneum, 1974.

VICKERY, JOHN B. *The Literary Impact of the Golden Bough.* Princeton, New Jersey: Princeton University Press, 1973.

———, ed. *Myth and Literature.* Lincoln, Nebraska: University of Nebraska Press, 1966.

WILLIAMS, SELMA R. *Demeter's Daughters: The Women Who Founded America.* New York: Atheneum, 1976.

———. *Kings, Commoners, and Colonists: Puritan Politics in Old & New England, 1603–1660.* New York: Atheneum, 1974.

Index